Texas Rules of Evidence
with Objections

Texas Rules of Evidence
with Objections

Third Edition

This third edition reflects changes to the Texas Rules of Evidence through January 1, 1999

Gerald Reading Powell
Professor of Law
Baylor Law School

Hon. Ed Kinkeade
United States District Court
Dallas, Texas

Anthony J. Bocchino
Jack E. Feinberg Professor of Litigation
Temple University Law School

David A. Sonenshein
I. Herman Stern Professor of Law
Temple University Law School

NATIONAL INSTITUTE FOR TRIAL ADVOCACY

Reproduction Permission
National Institute for Trial Advocacy
Notre Dame Law School
Notre Dame, Indiana
46556 (800) 225-6482 Fax (574) 271-8375
www.nita.org E-mail nita.1@nd.edu

Powell, Gerald Reading, Hon. Ed Kinkeade, Anthony J. Bocchino, and David A. Sonenshein, *Texas Rules of Evidence with Objections, Third Edition* (NITA, 2003).

ISBN 1-55681-811-4

Library of Congress Cataloging-in-Publication Data

Texas Rules of evidence with objections / Gerald Reading Powell ... [et al.].-- 3rd ed.
p. cm.
"This third edition reflects changes to the Texas rules of evidence through January 1, 1999."
Includes index.
ISBN 1-55681-811-4 (alk. paper)
1. Evidence (Law)--Texas. 2. Objections (Evidence)--Texas. I. Powell, Gerald Reading. II. National Institute for Trial Advocacy (U.S.) III. Texas. Supreme Court. Texas rules of evidence.
KFT1740.A4349P69 2003
347.764'06--dc21

2003045861

Contents

Objections
—A B C—

—D E F—

—G H—

—I J K—

—L M N—

—O P Q—

—R S—

Preface to

Texas Rules of Evidence with Objections, Third Edition

This text is designed to provide the practitioner and student with a convenient reference for raising trial objections and presenting responses.

The material is presented in alphabetical order. Tabs are located on the edges of the pages to aid in locating the appropriate section. Responses are found on the same pages/sections as the objections.

The cross-reference to the applicable Texas case law follows the objections and responses and an "Explanation" paragraph concludes each topic. This explanatory segment is designed to alert readers to a practice tip or legal interpretation crucial to proper understanding of the subject matter of that section.

This book is not designed to provide an in-depth analysis of evidentiary rulings or the application of the theories concerning the admission or exclusion of evidence. Instead, Texas Rules of Evidence with Objections was developed to furnish users with a complete reference of trial objections and responses, and is small enough to be easily carried to the courtroom or the classroom. We hope you find this material assists you in the pursuit of improving your litigation skills.

The Authors,

Gerald Reading Powell
Hon. Ed Kinkeade
Anthony J. Bocchino
David A. Sonenshein

Ambiguous Questions

A
B
C

Objection

- *Objection. The question is* (ambiguous) (vague).

Response

None recommended.

Cross-Reference to Texas Rule 611(a)

No Texas rule specifically covers forms of questions. The court has discretion to sustain the objection pursuant to Rule 611(a).

Explanation

This objection should only be made when, in the judgment of objecting counsel, the question will mislead the jury or witness to the detriment of counsel's client. The usual effect of such an objection is to make the opponent a better lawyer by forcing a more precise question. If, however, the jury is obviously confused by the question, the objection will communicate to the jury that objecting counsel is concerned with the ascertainment of truth in the trial process.

A likely response by a judge to this objection is to ask the witness if the witness understands the question. If the witness understands the question it will be allowed to stand. Otherwise, questioning counsel will be required to rephrase the question.

Argumentative Questions

Objection

- *Objection. The question is argumentative.*

Response

None recommended.

Cross-Reference to Texas Rule 611(a)

No Texas rule specifically covers forms of questions. The court has discretion to sustain the objection pursuant to Rule 611(a).

Explanation

This objection applies to questions on both direct and cross-examination. It may be appropriate where counsel attempts, in question form, to summarize the testimony of the witness, comment on the evidence, or draw inferences from the evidence. It is essentially jury argument during the questioning process. The propriety of this objection is largely subjective, depending on what the judge believes is appropriate, which will necessarily vary from court to court. The line between good, aggressive cross-examination and improper argumentative interrogation is a fine one.

A
B
C

Assuming Facts Not in Evidence

Objection

- *Objection. The question assumes a fact not in evidence. There has been no testimony that* (insert facts that have been assumed).

Responses

- *I will prove that fact in my next question.*
- *That fact has been proved during the earlier testimony of* (insert name of witness).
- *This fact will be proved during the testimony of* (insert name of witness).

Cross-Reference to Texas Rule 611(c)

Explanation

This objection should only be made when objecting counsel is confident that the witness cannot testify to the assumed fact. If the witness can testify to the assumed fact and questioning counsel knows how to ask the question, objecting counsel will be viewed by the jury as overly technical and attempting to hide the truth. In addition, by requiring questioning counsel to ask two questions instead of one, objecting counsel merely assists in making the opponent a better lawyer.

A
B
C

Authentication of Telephone Conversations and Voices

General Predicates

Personal Call; Witness Is Person Calling:

- *Did you have occasion to call* (name of person called)*?*
- *When did you make the call?*
- *How did you know what number to call?*
- *Who did you speak with?*
- *How do you know it was* (name of person called)*?*

Business Call; Witness Is Person Calling:

- *Did you have occasion to call* (name of business called)*?*
- *When did you make the call?*
- *How did you know what number to call?*
- *Who did you speak with?*
- *How do you know it was* (name of person speaking)*?*

A
B
C

- *Without, at this time, going into what was specifically said, what did the conversation generally concern?*

Personal or Business Call; Witness Is Person Called:

- *Did you receive a phone call* (at) (on) (general time of call)*?*
- *Who was it that called you?*
- *How do you know it was* (name of person calling)*?*

Voice Identification Predicate:

- *Do you have an opinion as to whose voice it was that you heard* (at) (on) (general time voice heard)*?*
- *What is your opinion?*
- *How do you know it was ________?*

Objection

- *Objection. The telephone conversation has not been authenticated because there is no proof of the identity of the person spoken to.*

A
B
C

Response

- *The identity of the participants in the telephone conversation has been established through the testimony of* (name of witness) *who testified that:*

  (a) *(he) (she) is familiar with and recognized the voice;* or

  (b) *(he) (she) called the number listed to* (name of participant), *and the other party identified himself as* (name of participant); or

  (c) *(he) (she) called the number listed to* (name of participant), *and the content of the conversation showed* (name of person) *to be the person who answered the call;* or

  (d) *(he) (she) called the number listed to* (insert name of business), *and the conversation related to business conducted by* (name of business) *over the telephone;* or

  (e) *where proved by a qualified expert witness (he) (she) has compared the voice in question with an authentic voice exemplar and (his) (her) opinion is that the voice in question is that of* (name of purported speaker).

Cross-Reference to Texas Rule 901

A
B
C

Explanation

The authentication of telephone conversations is usually accomplished through the testimony of one of the participants or other person who has gained familiarity with the voices of the participants and can give an opinion as to the identity of the persons speaking. Familiarity may be obtained either before or after the telephone conversation in question, so long as the circumstances of obtaining familiarity are sufficient to meet the quantum of proof required by Rule 104(b).

Telephone conversations which have been recorded can be authenticated by expert testimony consisting of comparison of the taped conversations with a voice exemplar by utilizing voice spectrography. Authentication can also come from any person who can demonstrate familiarity with the voice in question.

A
B
C

Authentication of Writings

General Authentication Predicates

Testimony of a Witness with Knowledge

After laying predicate of personal knowledge of writing:

- *I hand you what has been marked for identification as Exhibit ____. Can you identify it?*
- *What is it?*
- *Is Exhibit ____ the original or a copy?*
- (If document is the original) *Is Exhibit ____ in substantially the same condition as when you saw it* (on) (at) ________ (stating the time personal knowledge was acquired)?
- (If document is a copy) *Is Exhibit ____ a true and correct copy of _____ _____* (stating identity of the original document)?

Lay Opinion of Handwriting

- *Are you familiar with ________'s handwriting?*
- *How are you familiar with it?*

- *When did you become familiar with ________'s handwriting?*
- *I hand you what has been marked for identification as Exhibit ____. Do you have an opinion as to who wrote Exhibit ____?*
- *What is your opinion?*
- *What is the basis of your opinion?*

Expert Opinion of Handwriting

After establishing expertise and proving authenticity of exemplar, preferably by stipulation or admission:

- *I hand you what has been marked for identification as Exhibit ____. Have you previously had an opportunity to examine this handwriting exemplar?*
- *I now hand you what has been marked for identification as Exhibit ____. I will ask you to compare Exhibit ____ (exemplar) with Exhibit ____ (questioned document). Do you have an opinion as to whether or not these two exhibits were written by the same person?*
- *What is your opinion?*
- *What is the basis of your opinion?*

A
B
C

- *Based upon your training and experience, and your comparison of Exhibit ____ and Exhibit ____, do you have an opinion as to who wrote Exhibit ____?*
- *What is your opinion?*

Objection

- *Objection. This exhibit has not been authenticated.*

Responses

- *The instrument has been authenticated by:*
- *stipulation.*
- *the testimony of* ______ (name of witness) *who has testified that:*

  (a) *(he) (she) created the writing;* or

  (b) *(he) (she) was present at the creation of the writing and testified that it is in substantially the same condition as at the time of its creation;* or

  (c) *(he) (she) knows the handwriting because (he) (she) saw the author write or sign the instrument;* or

  (d) *(he) (she) knows the handwriting from having seen the author write or sign his signature at another time;* or

A
B
C

(e) *(he) (she) knows the handwriting by circumstantial evidence that shows* (state circumstances)*;* or

(f) *the testimony of* (expert witness) *who testified that (he) (she) has compared the handwriting in question with an authentic handwriting exemplar and that (his) (her) opinion is that the handwriting in question is that of* (name of purported author).

- *Your Honor, I request that you compare the handwriting in question with an admittedly authentic handwriting exemplar and find that it is the handwriting of* (name of purported author).

Cross-Reference to Texas Rules 901–903

Explanation

Authentication is a foundational requirement for the introduction of any writing. In most circumstances, counsel should attempt to prove authenticity pretrial—by stipulation or through a request for admission. If not done pretrial, authentication is proved easily by the testimony of a witness with knowledge of the authenticity of the writing.

A
B
C

In those situations where a witness with direct knowledge of identity or authorship is not available, authentication can normally be proved by circumstantial evidence. For example, in many business situations the receiver of a letter will not have ever actually seen his correspondent sign his signature. However, if business has been conducted on the basis of that signature in the past, that circumstance alone could be sufficient for authentication purposes.

It is important to note that the question of authentication is preliminary and to be decided by the judge utilizing the standard of proof provided in Rule 104(b). The proponent must merely put on some evidence sufficient to support a finding of authenticity. The judge is not free to make such a finding on conflicting evidence, but rather must admit the writing and let the jury decide whether or not it is authentic. Finally, because the issue of authenticity is one for determination under Rule 104(b), the predicate evidence going to the authenticity question must be itself admissible.

Best Evidence Rule

A
B
C

Objection

- *Objection. They are attempting to prove the content of* (writing in question) *in violation of the Best Evidence Rule as Exhibit ___ is not the original.*

Responses

- *The original's absence has been sufficiently accounted for, so secondary evidence is admissible because:*

  (a) *the original was shown to be lost or destroyed;* or

  (b) *the original cannot be obtained by any available judicial process or procedure;* or

  (c) *no original is located in Texas;* or

  (d) *the original is in the possession of* (opposing party against whom the contents are offered), *and they have failed to produce it though on notice by* (the pleadings) (or otherwise) *that the content of the document would be the subject of proof at trial;* or

A
B
C

(e) *the content of the writing is not closely related to a controlling issue, and so is collateral.*

- *This exhibit is considered to be an original under the Best Evidence Rule because:*

  (a) *it is a counterpart intended by (a person executing or issuing the exhibit) to have the same effect as an original;* or

  (b) *it is a negative or print of an original photograph;* or

  (c) *it is a printout from data stored in a computer and has been shown to reflect accurately the data stored.*

- *This exhibit is considered to be an admissible duplicate under the Best Evidence Rule because:*

  (a) *it is a counterpart produced by the same impression, or from the same matrix, as the original;* or

  (b) *it was produced (from a photograph) (by mechanical or electronic re-recording) (by chemical reproduction) (or other equivalent techniques which accurately reproduce the original) of the original.*

Cross-Reference to Texas Rules 1001–1009

Explanation

The original document rule, commonly known as the Best Evidence Rule, requires the proponent to offer the original of a document, photograph, or recording into evidence when the proponent seeks to prove its content, unless production is excused under the terms of the rule.

The Best Evidence Rule is only, however, a rule of preference. There are numerous qualifications to this rule. First, an original includes a counterpart intended by the executing persons to have the same effect as the original. Second, a duplicate (for example, a photocopy) is generally considered the equivalent of an original. Third, the original document rule has no application if the writing, recording, or photograph is collateral, that is, does not directly go to a controlling issue in the lawsuit.

Because the rule is merely a rule of preference for the original, the original need not be produced: where the original is lost or destroyed (not at the behest of

A
B
C

the proponent of the document); where the original cannot be obtained by judicial process; where no original is located within the state; or, where the original is in the control of the opponent and the opponent has been put on notice, by the pleadings or otherwise, that the contents of the document, recording, or photograph would be the subject of proof at trial.

The proponent of secondary evidence (that is, something other than the original) bears the burden of persuading the trial judge, pursuant to Rule 104, that the excuse for non-production is met. For example, the proponent can lay a predicate for the loss of the original by offering evidence of a diligent, but unavailing, search for the document.

—Character Evidence— Alleged Victim of Assaultive Conduct

Objection

- *Objection. The question calls for (the answer provides) evidence of character offered to show propensity.*

Response

- *This testimony is offered to show the character trait for (violence) (peacefulness) of* (specifying name of alleged victim of assaultive conduct) *pursuant to Rule 404(a)(2), on the issue of self-defense.*

Cross-Reference to Texas Rule 404(a)(2)

Explanation

In criminal cases this exception to the propensity rule applies to all types of prosecutions, except those which would be covered by Rule 412 (sexual assault, aggravated sexual assault, attempt to commit sexual assault, or aggravated sexual assault). Most commonly, it is invoked

A
B
C

when the defendant is charged with assaultive conduct, and the defendant alleges self-defense. In civil cases Rule 404(a)(2) permits a party accused of assaultive conduct, usually the defendant, to offer evidence, by way of opinion or reputation, regarding the victim's character for violence.

—Character Evidence— Character of the Accused Party

Objection

- *Objection. The question calls for (the answer provides) evidence of character offered to show propensity.*

Responses

- *This evidence is offered to show the character trait for* (specifying pertinent character trait) *of* (specifying name of party accused of conduct involving moral turpitude) *pursuant to Rule 404(a)(1).*
- *They have opened the door on character by offering evidence of the pertinent character trait.*

Cross-Reference to Texas Rule 404(a)(1)

Explanation

Criminal Cases

Rule 404(a)(1)(A) allows a defendant in any criminal case to offer character evidence, by reputation or opinion, as to his own good character, but only as to a pertinent

A
B
C

trait of character in the case. Thus, the defendant is allowed to prove that he would not likely commit this crime based on past behavior. The state is permitted to rebut with character evidence that shows the defendant's past actions show he likely did commit this crime.

Civil Cases

Rule 404(a)(1)(B) allows a party charged with conduct involving moral turpitude to oppose the charge with character evidence, by reputation or opinion witnesses, of the pertinent character trait for the purpose of showing his propensity not to engage in the conduct alleged.

Methods of Proof

A party's offer of character evidence under Rule 404(a)(1) is often called "putting character in issue." This is misleading because it might lead a party to believe it is proper to offer character evidence by way of specific instances of conduct under Rule 405(b). This is not permitted. Only opinion or reputation testimony is admissible under Rule 404(a)(1).

—Character Evidence— Other Wrongs or Acts

A
B
C

Objection

- *Objection. The question calls for (the answer provides) evidence of character offered to show propensity.*

Response

- *This evidence is offered, not to show propensity, but rather to prove:*

  (a) *motive, in that* (specifically explaining how motive is shown); or

  (b) *opportunity, in that* (specifically explaining how opportunity is shown); or

  (c) *intent, in that* (specifically explaining how intent is shown); or

  (d) *preparation, in that* (specifically explaining how preparation is shown); or

  (e) *plan, in that* (specifically explaining how plan is shown); or

  (f) *knowledge, in that* (specifically explaining how knowledge is shown); or

A
B
C

(g) *identity, in that* (specifically explaining how identity is shown); or

(h) *absence of mistake, in that* (specifically explaining how absence of mistake is shown); or

(i) *absence of accident, in that* (specifically explaining how absence of accident is shown); or

(j) *same transaction contextual evidence;* or

(k) *dangerousness of the (instrumentality) (premises), in that* (specifically explaining how dangerousness is shown).

Cross-Reference to Texas Rules 404 and 412 and Art. 38.37, Tex. Code Crim. Proc.

Explanation

Rule 404(b) is not an exception to the general rule forbidding the use of character evidence to show propensity. Rather, Rule 404(b) merely makes explicit what should be self-evident: evidence not offered to prove propensity is not excluded by the propensity rule. Rule 404(b) illustrates other purposes for such evidence that would not run afoul of the propensity rule.

Admissibility of evidence offered to prove one of these other purposes is actually determined under the ordinary relevance rules—Rules 401, 402, and 403.

Notice in Criminal Cases

The requirement of notice applies only in criminal cases, and only then if the defendant timely requests notice before trial. If notice is properly requested by the defendant, and the state desires to offer evidence under Rule 404(b) in its case-in-chief, then the state must provide it. A prosecutor's open file policy does not satisfy the notice requirement. The state need not give notice of rebuttal evidence or same transaction contextual evidence.

Character of the Accused in Sexual Assault Cases

Art. 38.37 of the Code of Criminal Procedure makes admissible prior crimes, wrongs, or acts committed by a defendant on a child under seventeen, where the crime involves the same child and the new crime is a sexual offense or an assault-type offense. The purpose is to allow the evidence to show the state of mind of the defendant or the prior relationship of the defendant and child.

A
B
C

—Character Evidence— Propensity Rule; Character as an Element of a Claim or Defense

Objection

- *Objection. The (question calls for) (answer provides) evidence of character offered to show propensity.*

Response

- *This evidence is offered, not to prove propensity, but rather to show character for* (specifying character trait at issue) *which is an essential element of our (claim) (defense) of* (specifying claim or defense).

Cross-Reference to Texas Rules 404 and 405

Explanation

Propensity Rule

Rule 404 states the general rule that evidence of a person's character is not admissible as proof that such person, whether or not a party, has acted in

A
B
C

conformity therewith. In other words, character evidence is generally inadmissible to prove propensity.

Rule 405 provides that character evidence may be proved, where relevant, by way of reputation or opinion evidence, and in more limited circumstances by specific instances of conduct.

"Have you heard" Questions

A character witness who testifies to reputation or opinion may be cross-examined concerning specific instances of conduct of the person about whom character evidence has been given, as long as the conduct is inconsistent with the testimony of the character witness. This cross-examination as to specific instances is admissible, not to attack the character of the person whose character is in issue, but rather to impeach the character witness. Such cross-examination is permissible on the theory that either the character witness has incomplete information on which to base the reputation, or the character witness has an inappropriate notion as to what constitutes good character.

A
B
C

Collateral Source Rule

Objection

- *May I approach the bench, Your Honor?* (At the bench) *Objection. The question violates the collateral source rule.*

Responses

- *Plaintiff opened the door to collateral source payments by testifying that* (specific testimony opening the door).

- *Collateral source benefits are relevant to impeach the plaintiff's testimony that* (specific testimony inconsistent with receipt of benefits).

Cross-Reference to Texas Rules 401, 402, and 403

There is no rule specifically addressing collateral source benefits, as there is for liability insurance under Rule 411. The common law collateral source rule is, however, now reflected in the relevance rules—401, 402, and 403.

A
B
C

Explanation

The collateral source rule excludes evidence that a plaintiff received any form of benefits, from some source other than the defendant, for the injuries which are the subject of the lawsuit. Examples of collateral sources include accidental injury insurance, disability insurance, worker's compensation insurance, private or government disability insurance, unemployment compensation, sick leave, or similar types of sources.

Though not codified when the rules of evidence were adopted, Texas courts continue to follow the common law collateral source rule. Under the rules, the basis for exclusion is the lack of relevance of collateral payments and the danger of unfair prejudice to the plaintiff if the jury believes that the plaintiff has already been compensated.

A
B
C

—Competence— Generally

Objection

- *Objection. This witness is incompetent to testify because he lacks the ability to* (specifying particular ground).

Response

- *The witness is presumed competent, and there has been no showing of any inability on the part of the witness to perceive, remember, communicate, or appreciate the oath. Any questions regarding the witness's testimonial capacities go to the weight of the evidence rather than the admissibility.*

Cross-Reference to Texas Rules 601–606

Explanation

"Competent" is the term applied to a person who possesses the abilities to serve as a witness in a trial or hearing. Competence embodies four qualities: perception, recollection, communication, and appreciation of the oath or affirmation.

The issue of competence is usually raised concerning child witnesses or witnesses who have a physical or mental deficiency. Rule 601 states that a witness is generally presumed competent to testify. Thus, unless challenged by the opponent or by the court on its own motion, a witness will be permitted to testify.

Insane Persons

A person who is insane at the time of his testimony, or at the time he perceived the relevant events, may be incompetent to testify. Not every insanity will render a witness incompetent. It must be the type of mental condition that interferes with the ability of the witness to perceive, to remember, to be truthful, or to accurately narrate what he knows.

Children

Children may be precluded from testifying because of an incompetence resulting from their age or maturity level. A child is incompetent if he or she does not have sufficient intellect "to relate transactions with respect to which they are interrogated." Rule 601(a)(2). A child who does not understand the obligation to testify truthfully would also be incompetent under this rule.

A
B
C

—Competence—
Dead Man's Rule

Objection

- *Objection. Under the Dead Man's Rule this interested (party) (witness) may not testify to uncorroborated oral statements of* (name of deceased or incompetent).

Responses

- *The Dead Man's Rule does not apply to this lawsuit because this is not an action by or against an executor, administrator, guardian, or the heirs or legal representatives of the decedent;* or
- *The Dead Man's Rule does not apply to this lawsuit because, though this is an action by or against the heirs or legal representatives of the decedent, it is not based in whole or in part on such oral statement;* or
- *The Dead Man's Rule does not apply to this witness because (he) (she) is neither a party nor a person who would be bound by a judgment in this case;* or

- *The Dead Man's Rule does not apply to non-party witnesses who have no interest in the lawsuit;* or
- *This witness will testify to an oral statement of* (name of deceased or incompetent), *which is corroborated by* (specifying already admitted corroborating evidence or yet-to-be offered corroborating evidence); or
- *Any objection under the Dead Man's Rule has been waived because (opposing party) called the witness to testify thereto by asking (him) (her)* (specifying question that waived Dead Man's Rule).

Request for Jury Instruction:

- *We request that the jury be instructed that* (name of witness) *is not permitted by the law to give evidence relating to any oral statement by the deceased or ward unless the oral statement is corroborated or unless the party or witness is called at the trial by the opposite party.*

Cross-Reference to Texas Rule 601

A
B
C

Explanation

The Dead Man's Rule is a rule of competence that prohibits a party or interested witness from testifying to uncorroborated oral statements by a deceased or insane person. The danger addressed by the rule is that the interested person will put words in the mouth of a person who cannot contradict the claimed statement because his lips are sealed by death or insanity.

The rule does not apply to every lawsuit. Rather, it must be a suit by or against an executor, administrator, or guardian, appearing in the suit in that capacity, and in which judgment may be rendered by or against such a person in that capacity. Rule 601(b) also applies to suits by or against the heirs or legal representatives of a decedent if the suit is based, at least in part, upon the objected-to oral statement.

Non-party witnesses, with no interest in the outcome of the case, are not restrained by this rule and may freely testify to oral statements, corroborated or not.

The rule does not exclude testimony about transactions with the deceased or incompetent, as the former statute did. Only oral statements by the deceased or incompetent are excluded.

A party whose testimony is excluded under this rule is entitled to a jury instruction as to the operation of the Dead Man's Rule.

A
B
C

—Competence—
Firsthand Knowledge

Objections

If there is no evidence of how witness knows matter inquired about:

- *Objection. There has been no showing that the witness has personal knowledge of* (specifying subject).

If there is evidence that witness does not have personal knowledge of matter inquired about:

- *Objection. The witness has no personal knowledge of* (specifying subject).

Responses

If there is no evidence of how witness knows matter inquired about:

- *I will lay the predicate at this time.*

If there is evidence that witness does have personal knowledge of matter inquired about:

- *We have shown that the witness has personal knowledge because he testified that* (specifying testimony).

If there is evidence both that witness does and does not have personal knowledge of matter inquired about:

- *The witness has shown that he has firsthand knowledge in that* (specifying basis of knowledge).
- *Under Rule 602 we only need to raise a fact issue of personal knowledge.*

Cross-Reference to Texas Rule 602

Explanation

A prerequisite of admissible testimony is the witness's possession of personal knowledge of the matter about which testimony is given. Generally, the proponent of the witness must lay a predicate on the issue of personal knowledge by offering sufficient evidence to support a finding that the witness has firsthand knowledge of the subject matter of his testimony.

Under Rule 602, the proponent need not convince the court by a preponderance of the evidence that the witness has personal knowledge. Rather, the proponent need only put on sufficient evidence to support a finding of personal knowledge.

—Competence— Juror Testimony

Objections

- *Your Honor, may I approach the bench?* (at the bench) *Objection. The witness may not testify because he is a juror. I move that the juror be excused;* or
- *Objection. The witness may not testify regarding any matter or statements occurring during deliberations on his or another juror's mental processes.*

Response

- *The witness will be testifying regarding an improper outside influence brought to bear on a juror.*

Cross-Reference to Texas Rule 606

Explanation

There is little occasion for testimony by jurors. Before adoption of this rule, jurors frequently gave testimony in support of jury misconduct claims. The rule makes it virtually impossible to prove jury misconduct. A juror is prohibited from testifying

A
B
C

to any occurrences or statements during deliberations. Nor may a juror testify to the effect of anything upon any juror's mind. The only matter a juror may now testify to is the existence of an outside influence upon a juror. Even this is limited, however, in that it must be someone not on the jury attempting to influence a juror. A juror bringing in outside information to influence the jury does not fall under this exception.

For purposes of Rule 606(b), "deliberations" means formal jury deliberations where the jury weighs the evidence in arriving at a verdict and does not refer to conversations between jurors during trial breaks or informal discussions among jurors during trial.

Compound (Multifarious) Questions

Objection

- *Objection. The question is multifarious.*

Response

None recommended

Explanation

The vice of a multifarious question lies in its tendency to confuse the jury regarding the testimony of the witness. When a witness answers "yes" to a question that asks about two separate subjects, it is impossible to know whether the witness is affirming the first query, the second, or both, and the potential for confusion is obvious.

As a rule, because multifarious questions are confusing, an objection will usually result in making the questioner a more effective advocate by clearing up the confusion counsel has created. Also, because the objection is easily met, the objection often gives the appearance that objecting counsel is hyper-technical. The objection, then, is best made only when the

A
B
C

multifarious question is likely to mislead the jury to the detriment of the objecting party.

A
B
C

Compromise and Offers of Compromise

Objection

- *Objection. This is evidence of compromise negotiations offered on liability or damages.*

Response

- *This evidence is admissible because:*

  (a) *the claim was not in dispute at the time of the compromise discussions;* or

  (b) *the evidence is not offered on liability or damages but to show (bias) (prejudice) (interest) (no undue delay) (an effort to subvert a criminal investigation).*

Cross-Reference to Texas Rule 408

Explanation

Compromise or settlement discussions are deemed inadmissible in order to encourage parties to settle disputed claims. Disclosure to the fact-finder of such evidence would chill compromise negotiations.

ABC

The rule forbids the admission of negotiations regarding *disputed* claims only. The term "disputed claim," however, does not refer only to claims reduced to litigation. A claim asserted outside of court proceedings, or disputed originally as to liability or amount, is disputed for purposes of the rule.

In addition, statements of fact, and indeed, any statements at all (not merely demands, offers, and counteroffers) made by the parties or their representatives in the course or context of compromise discussions, are inadmissible.

Of course, Rule 408 does not exclude facts, which though mentioned in the compromise negotiations, are otherwise discovered. More important, the rule does not bar the admission of compromise negotiations or statements made where offered for any relevant purpose other than proof of liability or damages. The rule expressly provides that such evidence is admissible to impeach a witness for bias, prejudice, or interest, to deny the opponent's claim of undue delay, or to show an attempt or effort to obstruct a criminal prosecution.

Rule 408 has no applicability to evidence of plea bargains or plea negotiations conducted in criminal cases. Such evidence is governed by Rule 410.

A
B
C

Cross-Examination Generally

Cross-Reference to Texas Rule 611

Explanation

Leading questions are not only permitted but expected on cross-examination. If the direct examination has, however, been conducted by leading questions under the adverse party or hostile witness rule, then the cross-examiner may be required to refrain from leading.

Cross-examination is not limited to the scope of the subject matter of direct examination as it is under the Federal Rules of Evidence. Cross-examination is wide open, limited only by concepts of relevance. Though there is no rule which specifically addresses recross-examination, a judge has the discretion to limit recross-examination to the scope of the redirect. However, just as redirect is rarely limited to the scope of the cross-examination, so too is recross generally free from restraint.

—Exhibits—
Demonstrative

General Predicate

After demonstrating personal knowledge of the matter depicted or represented:

- *I hand you what has been marked for identification as Exhibit ____. Can you identify it?*
- *What is it?*
- *Is Exhibit ____ a fair and accurate (depiction) (representation) of* (matter depicted or represented) *as of* (relevant time or date)?
- *Would it assist you in your testimony, or help the jury understand your testimony, if you had this exhibit available for your use?*

Objections

- *Objection. The exhibit has not been properly authenticated because there is no proof that it is a fair and accurate representation of (whatever it is offered to demonstrate).*
- *Objection. The exhibit contains hearsay. Specifically, it contains assertions that*

D E F

(specifying factual assertions). *Since the exhibit was made out of court, it is hearsay.*

DEF

Responses

- *The exhibit has been authenticated by the testimony of* (name of witness) *that it is a fair and accurate depiction of* (matter depicted) *as of the relevant date.*
- *We offer Exhibit ____ for demonstrative purposes only and not for the truth of the matter asserted.*

Cross-Reference to Texas Rule 901

Explanation

Demonstrative exhibits may also generally be utilized during opening statements as aids to persuasion. Counsel should obtain the court's permission beforehand, and such use of the exhibit would, of course, be subject to objection from the opponent. Such exhibits could also be used in argument, assuming they were admitted into evidence. Many judges, however, will not allow an exhibit into the jury room if it was admitted solely for demonstrative purposes.

—Exhibits—
Photographs and Videotapes

General Predicate

After demonstrating personal knowledge of the matter depicted as of the relevant date or time:

- *I hand you what has been marked for identification as Exhibit ____. Can you identify it?*
- *What is it?*
- *Is Exhibit ____ a fair and accurate depiction of* (matter depicted) *as of* (relevant date or time)*?*

Objections

- *Objection. The exhibit has not been properly authenticated because there is no proof that it is a fair and accurate depiction of* (stating what it is offered to depict).
- *Objection. The exhibit has not been properly authenticated because there is no proof that it is a fair and accurate depiction of* (stating what it is offered to depict) *at the time of* (stating relevant time).

Response

- *The exhibit has been authenticated by the testimony of* (name of witness) *that it is a fair and accurate depiction of* (matter depicted) *as of the relevant date.*

D
E
F

Cross-Reference to Texas Rule 901

Explanation

In modern day practice, photographs are typical exhibits in any case that involves a physical scene or object. The basic requirements for introduction of a photograph are that a witness with firsthand knowledge of the scene in issue testifies that the photograph shows a relevant view of a scene or object at a relevant time, and that it is a fair and accurate depiction of that scene, as of the relevant time.

Differences between what the witness saw at the relevant time and what the photograph shows usually will not mandate exclusion of the exhibit so long as the differences are acknowledged and the differences do not render the exhibit misleading.

—Exhibits—
Real Evidence

Predicate

After establishing personal knowledge of the object at the relevant time:

D
E
F

- *I hand you what has been marked for identification as Exhibit ____. Can you identify it?*
- *What is it?*
- *Is Exhibit ____ in substantially the same condition as it was when you saw it (on) (at)* (relevant date or time)*?*

Objection

- *Objection. There has been no showing of authenticity.*

Response

- *I have shown through the testimony of* (name of witness) *that he perceived the exhibit at a relevant time, that the exhibit is the one perceived, and that the exhibit is in substantially the same condition as it was at the relevant time.*

Cross-Reference to Texas Rule 901

D
E
F

Explanation

The process of admitting real evidence is essentially a process of authentication. Counsel must show that the object is the same tangible object observed by a witness at a relevant time. If the evidence is not distinctive, then it may be necessary to prove the chain of custody of the object to establish its authenticity.

It may also be important, depending upon the purpose of the offer, to show that it is in the same or similar condition as it was at the relevant time. If offered to show condition of the object at a relevant time, then chain of custody may be necessary.

—Exhibits—
Writings Generally

Objections

- *Objection. There has been no showing of relevance because* (stating specific reason).
- *Objection. Authenticity has not been shown.*
- *Objection. This exhibit violates the Best Evidence Rule.*
- *Objection. The exhibit is hearsay.*

Response

See chapters regarding relevance, authenticity, best evidence, and hearsay.

Cross-Reference to Texas Rule

Relevance is governed by Article IV, authenticity by Article IX, best evidence by Article X, and hearsay by Article VIII.

Explanation

Any time a writing is offered into evidence, four potential areas of objection must be considered: relevance, authentication, best evidence, and hearsay. In addition, because documents are capable of alteration, the judge will normally require testimony that an original document is in the same or similar condition as it was at a relevant time. If a copy of an original is admissible under the Best Evidence Rule, the proponent must prove that it is a true and correct copy.

Expert Opinion

Objections

D
E
F

- *Objection. The witness is not qualified to give opinions concerning* (specifying the relevant field of expertise).
- *Objection. This opinion is beyond the expertise in which the witness has been qualified.*
- *Objection. This opinion will not be helpful to jury determination or understanding of any fact in issue because* (specifying reasons, e.g., this issue is within the common understanding of laymen, and the jury is competent to decide the question on its own).
- *Objection. The question calls for a legal conclusion.*
- *Objection. The question calls for a conclusion on a mixed question of law and fact, and it is not based on proper legal concepts because* (specifying any legal term that has not properly been defined).
- *Objection. The question calls for an opinion that is unreliably based. It assumes facts that are contrary to the*

DEF

undisputed testimony in this case in that (explaining factual basis of opinion and testimony in the case). *This opinion is inadmissible under Rule 705(c) because the factual basis is insufficient for the opinion, and under Rule 403, because it has low probative value since the factual basis bears very little relation to the real and undisputed facts of this case. This low probative value is substantially outweighed by the danger that the jury will overvalue the opinion because it comes from a qualified expert and thereby be confused and misled, and by the danger of unfair prejudice because* (specifying nature of prejudice).

- *Objection. The question calls for an opinion that is unreliably based. It is not based upon valid principles of this field of expertise in that* (explaining unreliability of methodology). *This testimony is inadmissible under Rule 702 because it does not constitute scientific, technical, or specialized knowledge and would not be helpful to the jury in determining a fact in issue. The opinion sought is based upon a methodology that is not (scientifically) valid because:*

  (a) *it is not subject to testing for validity;* or

(b) *it relies upon the subjective interpretation of the expert;* or

(c) *it has not been published and was not subject to peer review by other experts in the field;* or

(d) *it has an unacceptable rate of error;* or

(e) *it is not a methodology generally accepted as valid by experts in this field;* or

(f) *it has no non-judicial uses, but rather was developed solely for purposes of this litigation.*

- *Objection. This opinion is inadmissible under Rule 403. It has low probative value since* (specifying reason probative value is low). *This low probative value is substantially outweighed by the danger that the jury will overvalue the opinion because it comes from a qualified expert and thereby be confused and misled, and by the danger of unfair prejudice because* (specifying nature of prejudice).
- *Objection. This opinion is based upon underlying facts that are inadmissible because* (specifying underlying facts and grounds of inadmissibility, e.g., hearsay). *We object to the opinion because there*

has been no predicate that such facts are reasonably relied upon by experts in the field, as required by Rule 703. In particular:

D E F

(a) *there is no showing that experts in this field customarily rely upon this type of facts or data;* or

(b) *there is no showing that reliance on these facts or data is reasonable. Specifically, it is unreasonable to rely upon unreliable facts, and the underlying facts or data relied upon here are unreliable because* (specifying reason for unreliability).

- *Objection. Though the expert's opinion may be based upon inadmissible facts, we object, under Rule 705(d), to the disclosure of those inadmissible facts to the jury. This opinion is based upon underlying facts that are inadmissible because* (specifying underlying facts and grounds of inadmissibility, e.g., hearsay). *Such facts are also inadmissible to show the expert's basis, under Rule 705(d), because the danger that they will be used for a purpose other than as explanation or support for the expert's opinion outweighs their value as explanation or support. Additionally, these facts are unfairly prejudicial because* (specifying nature of prejudice).

Responses

D
E
F

- *We have shown that the witness is qualified as an expert in* (field) *through (his) (her) knowledge, skill, experience, training, or education.*
- *We have shown that the area of expertise in which the witness is qualified is one that will be helpful to the jury in determining* (fact or conclusion in issue).
- *We have qualified the expert in the area of* (field), *and (his) (her) opinion is within that area.*

To objection to mixed question of law and fact:

- *An opinion on a mixed question of law and fact is proper. This question goes to the issue of ________, and I will be happy to define the term ________ for the witness.* (To the witness) *In answering this question concerning ________, the term ________, under the law of the State of Texas, means ________.* (Then ask question.)

DEF

To objection to insufficiency of basis:

- *The basis of this expert's opinion is* (specifying basis). *Any objection to the basis goes to the weight and not the admissibility of the opinion.*

To objection to disclosure of otherwise inadmissible basis:

- *This testimony has high probative value because it shows, in part, what this expert based the opinion on. We have a great need for this testimony because the jury will not give the opinion the weight it deserves if they believe that it is insufficiently based. The jury has a right to hear why this expert reached this conclusion. Furthermore, if the court is concerned about prejudice or confusion, then an instruction would eliminate that concern.*

Cross-Reference to Texas Rules 702–706

Explanation

Qualifications

There are no rigid requirements under the Texas rules for the qualifications of most experts. The rules do require, however, that the trial judge be persuaded that the purported expert has knowledge or training in an area of specialized knowledge beyond the abilities of the ordinary juror. The expert may be qualified because of education, training, professional experience, and/or knowledge gained in some other way. An expert must be qualified with regard to each opinion the expert is called on to provide.

Although an expert witness may possess knowledge, skill, expertise, or training, where the testimony supports a fact issue within the common knowledge of the jury, such testimony is properly excluded.

Basis of the Opinion

Pursuant to Rule 705, an expert will be permitted to testify as to his opinion whether or not he first testifies, or indeed ever testifies, as to the basis, supporting information, or data from which he reached that opinion, unless required to do so by the judge.

The 1998 amendment to Rule 705 adopted in civil cases a procedure for challenging the basis of an opinion that was previously

D
E
F

contained only in the criminal rules of evidence. The opponent may, under Rule 705(b), take the expert on voir dire examination to determine the adequacy of the underlying facts or data constituting the basis of the opinion.

Otherwise Inadmissible Basis

Pursuant to Rule 703, an expert is permitted to rely upon otherwise inadmissible evidence in reaching an opinion, so long as such evidence is reasonably relied upon by experts in that particular field to form opinions upon that subject. Rule 705(d) permits exclusion of an otherwise inadmissible factual basis that is offered under Rule 703 as a fact reasonably relied upon by experts in the field.

Scientific Opinions in Civil Cases—the *Robinson* Test

Rule 702 imposes a reliability standard—the *Robinson* test—on expert opinions. The reliability standard is derived from the helpfulness requirement of Rule 702, together with its reference to "scientific knowledge." That is, an opinion is not helpful knowledge unless it is based upon a reliable theory and technique. The following is a non-exclusive list of factors in determining reliability of scientific opinion evidence: (1) the extent to which the theory has been or can be tested; (2) the extent to which the technique relies upon the subjective interpretation of the expert; (3) whether the theory has been subjected to peer review and/or publication; (4) the technique's potential rate of error; (5) whether the underlying theory or technique has been generally accepted as valid by the relevant scientific community; and (6) the non-judicial uses which have been made of the theory or technique.

Scientific Opinions in Criminal Cases—the *Kelly* Test

The *Kelly* test has three requirements for meeting the clear and convincing standard. The scientific theory must be valid, the technique used must also be valid, and the technique must have been properly applied in this case.

The following nonexclusive factors should be considered by the trial court in determining reliability: (1) the extent that the theory and the technique are accepted in the scientific community; (2) the qualification of the expert; (3) the scientific literature supporting or attacking the theory or technique; (4) the technique's potential rate

DEF

of error; (5) the availability of other experts to evaluate the techniques; (6) the clarity with which evidence can be presented; and (7) the experience and skill of the person that applied the technique.

Mixed Questions of Law and Fact; Pure Questions of Law

Under Rule 704, a court will permit an expert to form an opinion for the trier of fact that embraces an ultimate issue to be decided by the fact-finder in the case. However, the opinion must be based upon proper legal concepts, that is, the question must embrace the same legal standards which the trier of fact will use to determine the fact question.

Form Objection Generally

Objection

- *Objection. The question is compound (or leading) (or seeks a narrative response).*

D E F

Response

Usually, the best response is to rephrase the question if it is a legitimate objection.

Cross-Reference to Texas Rule 611

Explanation

Objections to the form of a question usually have utility as a means of controlling opposing counsel. That is, they can be used to require opposing counsel to proceed in question-and-answer form, asking one clear question at a time, with answers on direct coming from the witness rather than counsel. Form objections have no utility either to exclude evidence totally or to preserve error for appeal.

D
E
F

The ruling on a form objection is purely a matter of judicial discretion. The court has authority to exercise its discretion to control the mode of interrogating witnesses under Rule 611(a).

Guilty Pleas, Offers of Pleas, and Related Statements

Objection

- *Objection. This evidence is inadmissible as a (withdrawn guilty plea) (nolo contendere plea) (withdrawn nolo contendere plea) (statement made as part of a plea hearing) (statement made as part of a plea negotiation).*

GH

Responses

- *This evidence is admissible because it is not being offered against the defendant who made the plea,* (specifying name of criminal defendant), *but rather against* (specifying party against whom offered).
- *This evidence is admissible, under the exception to Rule 410, because* (specifying name of opposing party) *opened the door to statements made in the plea (hearing) (negotiations) when testimony was offered that* (specifying testimony offered by opponent). *The offered evidence should be admitted because it ought in fairness be considered contemporaneously with the previously admitted evidence.*

Cross-Reference to Texas Rule 410

Explanation

This rule is an analogue to Rule 408 (Compromise and Offers to Compromise), except for the criminal settlement process. Evidence of the plea "and statements connected therewith" are inadmissible against the defendant who made the plea or who was a participant in the negotiations. Such evidence may be admissible, however, against someone other than such defendant.

G
H

In criminal cases a plea of nolo contendere is the equivalent of a guilty plea, and is admissible to the extent a guilty plea would be admissible. A withdrawn plea of nolo contendere is considered the same as a withdrawn guilty plea for admissibility purposes.

Habit and Routine Practice

Objection

After habit response to initial relevance objection:

- *I object that this evidence is irrelevant in that it is such an isolated occurrence as to be insufficient to constitute a habit or routine practice. There has been no showing of the frequency of the situation and the regularity of the response in order to constitute a habit under Rule 406.*

G H

Response

- *This evidence is relevant because it shows a consistent habit or routine practice which raises a permissible inference that the (party) (organization) likely acted in this case according to the habit or routine practice.*

Cross-Reference to Texas Rule 406

Explanation

By its nature, habit or routine practice testimony is circumstantial proof that certain conduct, or an act consistent therewith, occurred. Rule 406 represents a departure from the common law in two respects. First, Rule 406 allows habit and routine practice evidence even where there is firsthand or direct evidence of the event in question. Second, habit and routine practice evidence is admissible without corroborating evidence.

—Hearsay— Generally

Objections

- *Objection. The question calls for hearsay.*
- *Objection. The answer is hearsay as to what* (declarant) *said.*
- *Objection. The question calls for conduct hearsay because (*explaining why conduct was intended by declarant as a substitute for verbal expression).

G H

Response

- *The statement is not hearsay, because it is not being offered for the truth of the matter asserted, but rather to show the statement was made. The making of the statement is relevant:*

  (a) *because it is an operative fact or verbal act;* or

  (b) *because it has independent legal significance to prove (the existence of a contract) (a misrepresentation) (that a defamatory statement was made);* or

(c) *to show the knowledge or state of mind of* (person who heard the statement and whose knowledge or state of mind is somehow relevant in the case); or

(d) *to show notice to* (person or party whose conduct is in issue) *of* (existence of an event or condition); or

G
H

(e) *to show the information acted on by* (person whose conduct, knowing the information contained in statement, is somehow relevant in the case); or

(f) *to show a prior inconsistent statement made by this witness.*

Cross-Reference to Texas Rule 801

Explanation

Hearsay is an out-of-court statement, written or oral, that is offered to prove the truth of the matter asserted by the declarant of the statement. An out-of-court statement offered for any relevant purpose other than the truth of the matter asserted is non-hearsay. Thus, when the fact that an out-of-court statement was made is relevant, independent of whether the statement is true, the statement is non-hearsay.

—Hearsay—
Admissions of a Party Opponent

Objections

- *Objection. The question calls for hearsay.*
- *Objection. The answer is hearsay as to what* (declarant) *said.*

G H

Response

- *The statement is not hearsay, because:*

  (a) *the statement was made by the party opponent;* or

  (b) *though the statement was made by* (declarant) *it was adopted by the party opponent as (his) (her) own, and so is a vicarious admission of the party opponent;* or

  (c) *the statement was made by an agent authorized to speak on behalf of a party opponent, and so is a vicarious admission of the party opponent;* or

  (d) *the statement was made by an agent or servant of the party opponent, concerning a matter within the scope of the declarant's agency or employment, and was made during the existence of the declarant's agency or employment, and so is a vicarious admission of the party;* or

(e) *the statement was made by a co-conspirator of the party opponent, during the course of the conspiracy, and in furtherance of the conspiracy, and so is a vicarious admission of the party opponent.*

GH

Cross-Reference to Texas Rule 801(e)(2)

Explanation

Party admissions are statements made by a party that are offered by the opponent. The simplest form of admission is a statement made by the opposing party in either his individual or representative capacity. Rule 801(e)(2) further provides for a number of vicarious admissions. These are statements of a declarant other than the party opponent that are attributed to the party opponent because of the party's adoption of the statement or some relationship between the party opponent and the declarant.

—Hearsay—
Attacking and Supporting the Credibility of a Declarant

Objection

- *Objection. The question seeks to attack the credibility of a person who has not appeared as a witness.*

Response

- *This impeachment of an out-of-court declarant is permissible, under Rule 806, to the same extent available for a testifying witness.*

G
H

Cross-Reference to Texas Rule 806

Explanation

In most instances of the admission of an out-of-court statement, the declarant is considered a witness to the matters asserted out of court. Where such an out-of-court statement is admitted, the opponent may impeach the credibility of the absent declarant to the same extent that one could impeach a live witness. In other words, all of the usual impeachment methods are available.

G
H

—Hearsay— Depositions

Objections

- *Objection. The question calls for hearsay.*
- *Objection. The answer is hearsay as to what* (declarant) *said.*

Response

- *The statement is not hearsay because:*

  (a) *it was made in a deposition taken in this cause;* or

  (b) *it was made in a deposition taken in the same proceeding within the meaning of Rule 801(e)(3) of the Rules of Evidence and Rule 203.6(b) of the Rules of Civil Procedure, since the deposition was taken in a cause involving the same subject matter and was between the same parties or their representatives or successors.*

Cross-Reference to Texas Rule 801; Texas Rules of Civil Procedure 203.6 and 207

Explanation

Depositions are not treated as hearsay in Texas, as they are in federal court.

Any deposition taken in the same proceeding may be used at trial or hearing by any party, for any relevant purpose, against any party who was either present or represented at the deposition, or who had notice of it, or who substituted for such a party. A deposition is considered to be taken in the same proceeding if it falls under the definition of "same proceeding" found in Rule 203.6(b) of the Texas Rules of Civil Procedure. Therefore, not only are depositions considered non-hearsay if taken in the cause on trial, but also depositions are not hearsay if taken in any other cause, state or federal, provided that it involves the same subject matter and the same parties, their representatives, or successors.

—Hearsay—
Hearsay Within Hearsay

G
H

Objections

- *Objection. The question calls for hearsay within hearsay as to what* (second declarant) *stated that* (first declarant) *said.*
- *Objection. The answer is hearsay within hearsay as to what* (second declarant) *stated that* (first declarant) *said.*

Response

- *Both statements are admissible because each either comes within a hearsay exception or is non-hearsay. Specifically,* (explaining theory of admissibility as to each statement).

Cross-Reference to Texas Rule 805

Explanation

This is the multiple hearsay rule. The rule often applies to writings that contain attributed statements. To secure admission of the statement within the statement, the proponent must account for both out-of-court statements with either a hearsay exception or an argument that the out-of-court statement is not hearsay at all.

GH

—Hearsay—
Non-Hearsay Prior Statements of Witnesses

G H

Objections

- *Objection. The question calls for hearsay.*
- *Objection. The answer is hearsay as to what* (declarant) *said.*

Responses

- *The statement is not hearsay, pursuant to Rule 801(e)(1)(A), because it is inconsistent with the witness's trial testimony and was given under oath (at an earlier proceeding) (in a deposition).*
- *The statement is not hearsay, pursuant to Rule 801(e)(1)(B), because it is consistent with the witness's trial testimony and is offered to rebut an (express) (implied) charge of (recent fabrication) (improper influence or motive).*
- *The statement is not hearsay, pursuant to Rule 801(e)(1)(C), because it is a statement by the testifying witness of identification of a person made after perceiving such person.*

- *The statement is not hearsay, pursuant to Rule 801(e)(1)(D), because it is taken and offered in accordance with Code of Criminal Procedure article 38.071.*

Cross-Reference to Texas Rule 801(e)(1)

Explanation

It is not true, notwithstanding the number of lawyers and judges who believe it, that a statement is not hearsay just because the declarant is on the witness stand. Such statements, however, are defined as non-hearsay by Rule 801(e)(1). The Texas rules define as non-hearsay, however, the four categories of out-of-court statements contained in Rules 801(e)(1)(A)–(D). Such statements are admitted for the truth of the matter asserted. Each category of 801(e)(1) statements requires the declarant to be present and testifying in court and available for cross-examination. It is not necessary, however, that the declarant actually be on the stand at the time the prior statement is offered. It is enough that the declarant has already testified, but has not yet been excused. Such a declarant would be subject to cross-examination concerning the statement, because he or she could be recalled. The prior statement could therefore be proved up by another witness.

G
H

—Hearsay Exception— Absence of Entry in Business Records

Predicate Questions

If some records are offered—

Authentication Questions:

(a) *I hand you what has been marked for identification as Exhibit ____. Can you identify it?*

(b) *What is it?*

G H

Business Records Questions:

(a) *Were the records contained in Exhibit ____ made by, or from information transmitted by, a person with knowledge of the events or conditions recorded?*

(b) *Were these records made at or near the time of the events or conditions recorded?*

(c) *Were these records made in the regular course of your business?*

(d) *Were these records kept in the regular course of your business?*

Absence of Records Questions:

(a) *If* (event, act, or condition in question) *had occurred, would it have been recorded in the documents contained in Exhibit ____?*

(b) *Did you make a diligent search for records of ____________?*

(c) *Did you find any record of _______?*

G H

If no records are offered—

Business Records Questions:

(a) *Is it in the regular course of your business to make records of* (event, act, or condition in question)*?*

(b) *Is it in the regular course of your business to keep such records?*

(c) *Are such records made by, or from information transmitted by, a person with knowledge of the events or conditions recorded?*

(d) *Are such records made at or near the time of the events or conditions recorded?*

Absence of Records Questions:

(a) *Did you make a diligent search for records of ____________?*

(b) *Did you find any record of _______?*

Objections

- *Objection. The question calls for hearsay.*
- *Objection. The answer is hearsay as to what* (declarant) *said.*

G
H

Response

- *The absence of an entry in this record is admissible to show the nonoccurrence of an event pursuant to Rule 803(7).*

Cross-Reference to Texas Rules 803 and 902

Explanation

The absence of any entry concerning an event, which would ordinarily be recorded in a business record, may be offered to show that such event never occurred. The reliability of the absence of such entry lies in the notion that prudent, conscientious businesses regularly keep records of events that actually occur.

Such evidence is normally coupled with direct testimony from a witness with knowledge of the nonoccurrence of the event, but it may be independently sufficient evidence to support a verdict on the issue of the nonoccurrence of the event.

G
H

—Hearsay Exception— Absence of Public Record or Entry

Objections

- *Objection. The question calls for hearsay.*
- *Objection. The answer is hearsay as to what* (declarant) *said.*

G
H

Response

- *Evidence of a diligent but unavailing search of the records of the public agency or office is admissible pursuant to the hearsay exception contained in Rule 803(10).*

Cross-Reference to Texas Rule 803(10)

Explanation

As with Rule 803(7), this rule provides a hearsay exception for evidence of the absence of a record or record entry. The proof which the rule contemplates is evidence of a diligent but unavailing search of the records or record-keeping system of a public office or agency that regularly maintains such records.

—Hearsay Exception— Excited Utterance

G
H

Objections

- *Objection. The question calls for hearsay.*
- *Objection. The answer is hearsay as to what* (declarant) *said.*

Response

- *This statement is admissible under the excited utterance exception.*

Cross-Reference to Texas Rule 803(2)

Explanation

Excited utterances gain their reliability from the connection between the making of the statement and the startling event. Thus, to qualify as an excited utterance, the event that gives rise to the statement relating to it must be sufficiently startling so as to remove the likelihood of self-serving reflection in the making of the statement.

Unlike present sense impressions, an excited utterance need not be contemporaneous with the pertinent event. Texas cases have held a statement to be admissible under this exception even though there was a passage of many minutes or even hours between the event and the statement. The critical element is not time, but whether the declarant was still acting under the stress of the exciting or startling event when the statement was made.

—Hearsay Exception— Family Records

Objections

- *Objection. The question calls for hearsay.*
- *Objection. The answer is hearsay as to what* (declarant) *said.*

G
H

Response

- *This statement is admissible under the family record exception.*

Cross-Reference to Texas Rule 803(13)

Explanation

The reliability of these writings stems from the fact that an entry in such a document or item would not be made erroneously without family or personal protest. There is no requirement of contemporaneity of entry for family records. Such writing must, however, like any other, be authenticated. The rule does away with the common law predicate that the declarant be unavailable, be a family member, have no motive to fabricate, and have made the statement ante litem motam.

—Hearsay Exception— Former Testimony

Objections

- *Objection. The question calls for hearsay.*
- *Objection. The answer is hearsay as to what* (declarant) *said.*

Response

- *This statement is admissible under the former testimony exception.*

G H

Cross-Reference to Texas Rule 804

Explanation

This exception draws its reliability from the general lack of hearsay dangers at the time the statement was made. The former testimony, now an out-of-court statement, was made under oath and the person against whom it is now offered, or someone in a similar position in a civil case, had the opportunity to examine and confront the witness with a similar motive.

G
H

—Hearsay Exception— Judgment as to Personal, Family or General History, or Boundaries

Objection

- *Objection. The document is an out-of-court statement offered for its truth and is therefore hearsay.*

Response

- *This statement is admissible as a judgment as to personal, family or general history, or boundaries pursuant to Rule 803(23).*

Cross-Reference to Texas Rule 803(23)

Explanation

This exception provides a means to prove a fact essential to an earlier judgment as to personal, family, or general history, or as to boundaries. This rule must be read in conjunction with Rules 803(19) and 803(20), because Rule 803(23) only permits the admissibility where the judgment proves facts that would be provable by reputation evidence.

G H

—Hearsay Exception— Judgment of Previous Conviction

G
H

Objections

- *Objection. The question calls for hearsay.*
- *Objection. The answer is hearsay as to what* (declarant) *said.*

Response

- *This statement is admissible as a judgment of previous conviction pursuant to Rule 803(22).*

Cross-Reference to Texas Rule 803(22)

Explanation

The exception provides for the admission of prior felony convictions for the truth of facts essential to the judgment of conviction. Such conviction is admissible for its truth in a second case only against the person convicted in a first case. A no contest plea may not be admitted under this exception.

If the conviction is still on appeal, then it is not admissible under this exception.

In criminal cases evidence of any prior conviction to prove an element in the present case is admissible regardless of the plea, if it is a prior conviction of the accused in the present case. The purpose of the rule is to allow collateral estoppel of some fact proven in the prior case, and necessary to prove the present case. If the conviction is of someone other than the accused, the exception does not apply. If the third party's conviction is an element of the new case, then this rule would be applicable, as in the case of committing an offense by dealing with a felon. Proof of the conviction of that felon would fall under this rule.

G
H

—Hearsay Exception— Learned Treatises

Objection

- *Objection. The document is an out-of-court statement offered for its truth and is therefore hearsay.*

Response

- *This statement is admissible under the learned treatise exception.*

Cross-Reference to Texas Rule 803(18)

Explanation

Under the learned treatise exception to the hearsay rule, a court may admit passages, excerpts, or on occasion, the entire contents of a book, article, or other writing on a subject ordinarily the subject of expert testimony. The learned treatise, or parts thereof, are only to be admitted when used to cross-examine an expert witness or when an expert witness has relied upon a learned treatise in the direct examination. Significantly, the treatise may be admitted for its substantive truth, whether offered during direct or cross.

G
H

—Hearsay Exception— Market Reports and Commercial Publications

Objection

- *Objection. The document is an out-of-court statement and therefore hearsay.*

G
H

Response

- *This statement is admissible as a market report or commercial publication pursuant to Rule 803(17).*

Cross-Reference to Texas Rule 803(17)

Explanation

Market reports or quotations and commercial publications, including commercial newspapers, actuarial papers, and the like, are admissible against a hearsay objection. They gain their reliability from the general reliance placed on them by the entities that use them. As a result, the person or entity that creates such documents for use in a business or profession has an incentive to make the documents reliable and accurate. In addition, any inaccuracies are likely to be corrected. The predicate of use and reliance may be proved by a person with knowledge of the particular occupation, including an expert.

G
H

G
H

—Hearsay Exception— Marriage, Baptismal, and Similar Certificates

Objection

- *Objection. The document is an out-of-court statement offered for its truth and is hearsay.*

Response

- *This statement is admissible as a marriage, baptismal, or similar certificate pursuant to Rule 803(12).*

Cross-Reference to Texas Rule 803(12)

Explanation

This hearsay exception admits the facts relating to religious ceremonies, such as marriages or baptisms, so long as the entrant is authorized by law or religious practice to perform such ceremony, and the record is made contemporaneously with or reasonably soon after the occurrence of the ceremony.

These records are considered to be reliable because of the solemnity of the occasion, the entrant's legal authorization, and the contemporaneity of the entry with the fact or ceremony recorded.

G H

G
H

— Hearsay Exception— Present Sense Impression

Objections

- *Objection. The question calls for hearsay.*
- *Objection. The answer is hearsay as to what* (declarant) *said.*

Response

- *This statement is admissible under the present sense impression exception, Rule 803(1).*

Cross-Reference to Texas Rule 803(1)

Explanation

Present sense impressions gain their reliability from the virtual contemporaneity of the making of the out-of-court statement and the occurrence of the event described or explained. The substantial contemporaneity of the event and the statement negate the likelihood of deliberation or conscious misrepresentation.

Another potential credibility defect, lapse of memory, is likewise minimized by the short time period between the perception and statement.

G
H

—Hearsay Exception— Public Records and Reports

Objections

- *Objection. The question calls for hearsay.*
- *Objection. The answer is hearsay as to what* (declarant) *said.*
- (In a criminal case) *Objection. The report is not admissible against a criminal defendant.*

Response

- *The statement is admissible under the hearsay exception for public records and reports.*

Cross-Reference to Texas Rule 803(8)

Explanation

Public records or reports gain their reliability from the public duty or the duty imposed by law on the maker to observe and record the kinds of events contained in such public records or reports. In addition, the maker of the record or report will have no interest in reporting or recording information favoring one side over another. There are three types of matters which are admissible under the public records exception:

(a) records or reports that disclose the activities of the public agency;

(b) observations made pursuant to legal duty and which the public official has a legal requirement to record; or

(c) factual findings (including conclusions and opinions derived therefrom) which result from an investigation made pursuant to law.

G
H

—Hearsay Exception— Recorded Recollection

Objections

- *Objection. The question calls for hearsay.*
- *Objection. The answer is hearsay as to what* (declarant) *said.*

Response

- *This statement is admissible under the past recollection recorded exception.*

Cross-Reference to Texas Rule 803(5)

Explanation

The predicate for past recollection recorded is the following:

(a) the witness must have a failure of recollection while on the witness stand;

(b) the witness must authenticate a memorandum;

(c) the memorandum must contain facts of which the witness testifies he once had personal knowledge;

(d) the memorandum must have been created or adopted by the witness at a time when the matter was fresh in the witness's memory; and

(e) the memorandum must accurately reflect the witness's knowledge.

G H

—Hearsay Exception— Records of Documents Affecting an Interest in Property

Objection

- *Objection. The document is an out-of-court statement offered for its truth and is therefore hearsay.*

G
H

Response

- *This statement is admissible as a record of a document affecting an interest in property pursuant to Rule 803(14).*

Cross-Reference to Texas Rule 803(14)

Explanation

The record of a document of the type described in this rule is admissible for its truth in regard to the contents of the original recorded document, as well as for the fact of its execution and delivery by the parties to the document. These documents are considered to be reliable, because they are records of a type kept by a public office, such as a registry of deeds, pursuant to recording statutes.

—Hearsay Exception— Records of Regularly Conducted Activity: Business Records

Predicate Questions

Authentication Questions:

(a) *I hand you what has been marked for identification as Exhibit ____.*

(b) *Can you identify it?*

(c) *What is it?*

G H

Business Records Questions:

(a) *Were the records contained in Exhibit ____ made by, or from information transmitted by, a person with knowledge of the events or conditions recorded?*

(b) *Were these records made at or near the time of the events or conditions recorded?*

(c) *Were these records made in the regular course of your business?*

(d) *Were these records kept in the regular course of your business?*

Objections

- *Objection. The exhibit is hearsay.*
- *Objection. The exhibit contains hearsay within hearsay, specifically for example* (specifying at least one example of a double hearsay statement).

Response

- *This exhibit is admissible under the business record exception.*

G
H

Reply

- *This exhibit does not qualify as a business record because:*

  (a) *it was made solely for litigation purposes, and therefore was not made in the regular course of business, and is not trustworthy.*

  (b) *the (sources of information) (method or circumstances of preparation) indicate a lack of trustworthiness.*

  (c) *the record is hearsay within hearsay since it contains statements by* (declarant) *who was not under a business duty to report to* (entity that made record).

Cross-Reference to Texas Rules 803(6), 803(8), and 902(10)

Explanation

A business record gains its reliability from the regularity of the record-keeping operation which is necessary for the transaction of regularly conducted activity. The exception is premised on the notion that if the record is good enough to rely upon for business purposes, then it ought to be reliable enough for admission into evidence when issues regarding the business are litigated.

The rule applies to the records of any business, institution, association, profession, or occupation. Whether the entity in question has a profit motive for its existence is irrelevant.

G
H

—Hearsay Exception— Records of Religious Organizations

Objection

- *Objection. The record is an out-of-court statement offered for its truth and is hearsay.*

Response

- *This statement is admissible as a record of a religious organization pursuant to Rule 803(11).*

Cross-Reference to Texas Rule 803(11)

Explanation

This exception for regularly kept records of personal or family history gains its reliability from the fact that such events are ordinarily contemporaneously recorded by a religious functionary or clergyman with no motive to falsify a record on which persons ordinarily rely.

Though bearing some superficial similarity to business records under Rule 803(6), there is no requirement that the entry be contemporaneous to the event recorded, or that the entrant have personal knowledge or a source with personal knowledge.

G
H

—Hearsay Exception— Records of Vital Statistics

Objection

- *Objection. The record is an out-of-court statement offered for its truth and is hearsay.*

GH

Response

- *The statement is admissible pursuant to Rule 803(9) for records of vital statistics.*

Cross-Reference to Texas Rule 803(9)

Explanation

Records of vital statistics gain their reliability from the circumstances of their making. Ordinarily, the information contained in such records is provided by doctors or other persons who have no interest in the outcome of any future litigation. Furthermore, they are recorded by public officials who have an official duty to receive, record, and maintain such records.

—Hearsay Exception— Reputation as to Character

Objections

- *Objection. The question calls for hearsay.*
- *Objection. The answer is hearsay as to what* (declarant) *said.*

G H

Response

- *This statement is admissible as reputation as to character pursuant to Rule 803(21).*

Cross-Reference to Texas Rule 803(21)

Explanation

Reputation is a collection of hearsay. It must be reported by a witness on the stand who has had occasion to overhear discussion of the person's character, either among such person's associates or among people in the community. Reputation is distinguished from opinion on the question of character because opinion raises no hearsay problems, but merely refers to a notion formed by the witness from personal experience.

GH

—Hearsay Exception— Reputation Concerning Boundaries or General History

Objections

- *Objection. The question calls for hearsay.*
- *Objection. The answer is hearsay as to what* (declarant) *said.*

Response

- *This statement is admissible as a statement of reputation concerning boundaries or general history pursuant to Rule 803(20).*

Cross-Reference to Texas Rule 803(20)

Explanation

Reputation concerning boundaries or general history, though a collection of hearsay statements, is admissible under this exception so long as the reputation arose prior to the controversy involved in the trial, and the witness is familiar with the reputation, having heard it discussed in the relevant community.

—Hearsay Exception— Reputation Concerning Personal or Family History

Objections

- *Objection. The question calls for hearsay.*
- *Objection. The answer is hearsay as to what* (declarant) *said.*

G H

Response

- *This statement is admissible as a statement of reputation concerning personal or family history pursuant to Rule 803(19).*

Cross-Reference to Texas Rule 803(19)

Explanation

Reputation concerning personal or family history is admissible against a hearsay objection so long as it is generally accepted among the family, associates, or community where the reputation is known. The witness who testifies concerning the reputation must be familiar with that reputation, which is shown by (a) his being a member of the relevant family, community, or group of associates, and (b) the witness's familiarity with the reputation, having either heard it discussed or taken part in such discussions.

—Hearsay Exception— Requirement of Unavailability

Objections

- *Objection. The question calls for hearsay.*
- *Objection. The answer is hearsay as to what* (declarant) *said.*

G H

Response

- *The declarant is unavailable because (he) (she):*

  (a) *was exempted from testifying concerning the subject of the statement by ruling of the court on the ground of privilege;* or

  (b) *persists in refusing to testify concerning the subject of the statement, despite a court order to do so;* or

  (c) *testified to a lack of memory on the subject of the statement;* or

  (d) *is unable to testify at the hearing because of (death) (illness)*; or

  (e) *is absent from the hearing, and we have been unable to procure (his) (her) attendance through process or other means.*

Cross-Reference to Texas Rule 804

Explanation

Rule 804(b) exceptions require the declarant's unavailability. The types of unavailability listed in Rule 804(a) are not the exclusive circumstances of unavailability. Rather, Rule 804(a) lists circumstances which per se amount to unavailability, but the rule does not preclude any other legitimate showing of unavailability that the trial judge determines acceptable pursuant to Rule 804.

G H

If the proponent relies upon the fifth type of unavailability, absence from the hearing, the predicate must include proof that the proponent could not compel the declarant to attend the hearing, nor could the declarant be deposed ("attendance or testimony").

—Hearsay Exception— State of Mind

Objections

- *Objection. The question calls for hearsay.*
- *Objection. The answer is hearsay as to what* (declarant) *said.*

Responses

- *This statement is admissible under the state of mind exception.*
- *Even though the statement looks backward in time, it is permissible because it relates to the execution, revocation, identification, or terms of the declarant's will.*

Objecting Party's Reply

- *The state of mind exception is not applicable because:*

  (a) *the statement looks backward in time, and so is not a then existing state of mind;* or

  (b) *the declarant's state of mind is not relevant;* or

G H

(c) *the statement does not go to the declarant's state of mind.*

- *Even if admissible under the state of mind exception the statement is admissible only to prove that* (declarant) *believed* (fact stated by declarant), *and not to prove that* (fact stated by declarant) *is true.*

GH

If Statement Admitted Over This Objection:

- *We request that the jury be instructed that it may consider this statement only as proof that* (declarant) *believed* (fact stated by declarant), *but not that* (fact stated by declarant) *is true.*

Cross-Reference to Texas Rule 803

Explanation

Statements of then existing mental or emotional condition gain their reliability from the contemporaneity of the statement and the state of mind, sensation, or condition that is described by the declarant. It is critical to note that only statements regarding a *present* (at the time of the making of the statement) mental or emotional condition fit within the exception. A statement regarding a past condition will not be admissible, because there is no substantial guarantee of reliability. That is, the time between the existence of the condition of mind and the statement allows the declarant time for reflection and fabrication.

—Hearsay Exception— Statement Against Interest

Objections

- *Objection. The question calls for hearsay.*
- *Objection. The answer is hearsay as to what* (declarant) *said.*

G
H

Response

- *This statement is admissible as a statement against interest pursuant to Rule 803(24).*

Cross-Reference to Texas Rule 803(24)

Explanation

Civil Cases

A statement against interest is an out-of-court declaration that was so far against the interest of the declarant when he made it that he would not have made the statement unless it was true. This guarantee of reliability is what justifies this hearsay exception. Unlike the corresponding federal rule, unavailability of the declarant is not required.

The key to this exception is whether a reasonable person would make such a statement if it was untrue. The circumstances surrounding the making of the statement usually determine its admissibility.

Criminal Cases

This exception is often confused with a simple admission by a defendant. An admission by a criminal defendant is not hearsay, does not fall under this exception, and thus requires no corroboration. This rule covers a statement by someone other than the accused that admits to some crime and implicates the defendant in so doing. Before that statement is admissible against the accused: (1) the declarant must implicate himself as well as the accused; (2) there must be a high degree of independent corroboration; and (3) the statement must not be offered in a joint trial of the declarant and accused.

G
H

—Hearsay Exception— Statement of Personal or Family History

Objections

- *Objection. The question calls for hearsay.*
- *Objection. The answer is hearsay as to what* (declarant) *said.*

Response

- *This statement is admissible as a statement of personal or family history pursuant to Rule 804(b)(3).*

Cross-Reference to Texas Rule 804(b)(3)

Explanation

This exception gains its reliability from the fact of the declarant's likely reliance on such information throughout the course of the declarant's life. The requirement of the declarant's personal knowledge, which ordinarily must be apparent from the circumstances of the making of a declarant's admissible hearsay statement, is explicitly dispensed with pursuant to Rule 804(b)(3).

—Hearsay Exception— Statement under Belief of Impending Death

Objections

- *Objection. The question calls for hearsay.*
- *Objection. The answer is hearsay as to what* (declarant) *said.*

G H

Response

- *This statement is admissible under the dying declaration exception.*

Cross-Reference to Texas Rule 804(b)(2)

Explanation

A statement made under belief of impending death gains its reliability from the notion that a declarant, who in good faith believes that he is about to die, would not fabricate either the cause of death or the circumstances that caused the declarant's condition. The rule does not require a declarant to die as a requirement for admission of a statement under belief of impending death. The guarantee of reliability is found in the reasonable *belief* on the part of the declarant that he is about to die.

G
H

—Hearsay Exception— Statements for Purposes of Medical Diagnosis or Treatment

G H

Objections

- *Objection. The question calls for hearsay.*
- *Objection. The answer is hearsay as to what* (declarant) *said.*

Response

- *This statement is admissible as a statement for purposes of medical diagnosis or treatment pursuant to Rule 803(4).*

Objecting Party's Reply

- *This exception is not applicable because the statement is not pathologically germane, that is, reasonably pertinent to diagnosis or treatment.*
- *This exception is not applicable because the statement was made by the (doctor, nurse, paramedic, etc.), rather than to (him/her).*

Cross-Reference to Texas Rule 803(4)

Explanation

Statements made for purposes of medical diagnosis or treatment gain their reliability from the notion that one who is seeking medical treatment has a strong interest in being truthful to a person who is in the position to render or obtain medical assistance. This would include, of course, statements to any medical professional, as long as diagnosis or treatment is sought by the patient.

G H

Statements of causation or the external source of the physical condition mentioned in the out-of-court statement will only be admissible if pertinent to the medical diagnosis or treatment. If the statement is not related to what a doctor needs to know for proper diagnosis or treatment, then the declarant lacks the incentive to be truthful.

—Hearsay Exception— Statements in Ancient Documents

Objection

- *Objection. This statement is contained in an out-of-court writing offered for its truth, which is hearsay.*

G H

Response

- *This statement is admissible under the ancient document exception.*

Cross-Reference to Texas Rules 803(16) and 901(b)(8)

Explanation

Statements contained in ancient documents gain their reliability from the notion that a document created twenty or more years prior to its being offered during litigation is unlikely to be created at a time when there was any motive to falsify such document, at least for purposes of the current litigation. Rule 803(16) is unusual in that it states in its terms a requirement of authenticity. Thus, there is a direct tie-in between Rule 803(16) and the authentication provision of Rule 901(b)(8), which provides a predicate for authenticity of an ancient document. That predicate requires the following showing:

(a) the condition of the document creates no suspicion regarding its authenticity;

(b) the document has been kept in a place where it likely would be kept if it were authentic; and

(c) it has indeed been in existence for at least twenty years at the time of its offer.

—Hearsay Exception— Statements in Documents Affecting an Interest in Property

Objection

- *Objection. The document is an out-of-court statement offered for its truth and is therefore hearsay.*

Response

- *This statement is admissible pursuant to Rule 803(15) as a statement in a document affecting an interest in property.*

Cross-Reference to Texas Rule 803(15)

Explanation

While Rule 803(14) is limited to the proof of the content of the officially recorded document, Rule 803(15) is broader. It permits the admission of statements contained in a document, whether or not recorded, which create, relate to, or affect an interest in property. There are two requirements for admissibility. First, the factual statement contained in the document must relate or be relevant to the purpose of the document. Second, the document would only be admissible so long as dealings with the property after the time that the document was created have not been inconsistent with the truth of the statement or the purport of the document offered.

GH

—Hearsay Exception— Then-Existing Physical Condition

Objections

- *Objection. The question calls for hearsay.*
- *Objection. The answer is hearsay as to what* (declarant) *said.*

G H

Response

- *This statement is admissible as a statement of a then existing physical condition pursuant to Rule 803(3).*

Objecting Party's Reply

- *The state of physical condition exception is not applicable, because:*

  (a) *the statement looks backward in time, and so is not a then existing physical condition;* or

  (b) *the declarant's physical condition is not relevant.*

Cross-Reference to Texas Rule 803(3)

G
H

Explanation

A statement of a then existing physical condition gains its reliability from the contemporaneity of the statement and the existence of the physical condition described by the declarant. It is critical to note that only statements regarding present (at the time of the making of the statement) physical conditions come within the exception. A statement regarding a past condition will not be admissible, because there is no substantial guarantee of reliability. That is, the time between the existence of the bodily condition and the statement allows the declarant time to reflect and fabricate.

Statements that qualify for admissibility pursuant to Rule 803(3) need not be made to a physician and need not be made for purposes of obtaining medical diagnosis or treatment.

—Impeachment— Generally

Objections

To an attempt to impeach a witness called by the impeaching party, with an otherwise inadmissible hearsay statement:

- *Objection. The question calls for hearsay.*

If offered for impeachment purposes:

- *Objection. Counsel has called this witness for the primary purpose of impeaching him with an otherwise inadmissible hearsay statement. We object under Rule 403. Probative value is very low because the proponent has no need for the evidence since they created their own need for the impeachment by calling the witness to testify. This low probative value is substantially outweighed by the danger that the jury will be confused and misled to take the statement for the truth of the matter asserted, despite a limiting instruction.*

Responses

To an objection that the witness was called for the primary purpose of impeachment with otherwise inadmissible hearsay:

- *This witness was not called for the primary purpose of impeachment. He was called to testify concerning* (specifying non-impeachment purposes). *Since he may properly testify to these matters, we may impeach him on other matters which he will testify about, and we are entitled to impeach our own witness under Rule 607.*

I
J
K

Cross-Reference to Texas Rules 607 and 403

Explanation

Rule 607 represents a major departure from the common law by eliminating the common law voucher rule.

Some Texas courts, as well as the U.S. Court of Appeals for the Fifth Circuit, have held that a party may not call a witness for the sole or primary purpose of impeaching that witness with otherwise inadmissible evidence. Since Rule 607 does not expressly contain any such limitation upon impeachment, the objection is probably best made under Rule 403. That is, probative value is low since the evidence is offered only for the limited purpose of impeachment, and the proponent himself created the need for the impeachment by calling the witness in the first place. On the other hand, there is a danger that the jury may be confused or misled and take the evidence for its forbidden hearsay purpose, even though there is a limiting instruction. Of course, if the impeaching party can show other legitimate purposes for calling the witness, then that party will probably be allowed also to impeach under Rule 607.

—Impeachment— Bias, Prejudice, Interest, and Improper Motive

Objections

To question posed on cross-examination:

- *Objection. This is irrelevant because* (stating specific reasons testimony is irrelevant).
- *Objection. Counsel has not laid proper predicate, because the witness has not been advised of the circumstances supporting the claim of (bias) (prejudice) (interest) (improper motive).*

I
J
K

If bias or interest based upon prior statements of witness:

- *Objection. Counsel has not laid the proper predicate, because the witness has not been advised of where, when and to whom the statements were made.*
- *Objection. Counsel has not laid the proper predicate, because the witness has not been advised of the content of the statements.*

To extrinsic evidence:

- *Objection. This testimony is irrelevant because the witness has not yet testified, and so (his) (her) credibility is not in issue.*
- *Objection. Counsel has not laid the proper predicate for use of extrinsic evidence to impeach, because the witness was not confronted with the alleged (bias) (prejudice) (interest) (improper motive) on cross-examination.*
- *Objection. Extrinsic evidence is inadmissible to impeach, because the witness was confronted with the alleged (bias) (prejudice) (interest) (improper motive), and unequivocally admitted its existence.*

If bias or interest based upon prior statements of witness:

- *Objection. Counsel has not laid the proper predicate for use of extrinsic evidence to impeach, because the witness was not advised of where, when, and to whom the statements were made.*

- *Objection. Counsel has not laid the proper predicate for use of extrinsic evidence to impeach, because the witness was not advised of the content of the statements.*

Responses

To an objection posed to cross-examination:

- *I am attempting to show that the witness has (a bias) (a prejudice) (an interest in the outcome of the case) (an improper motive for testifying) because* (stating specific basis).

I
J
K

To an objection posed to extrinsic evidence, where the witness with the alleged bias, prejudice, interest, or improper motive has not already testified:

- *The witness will probably testify since (he) (she) has been listed by my opponent, and I offer this evidence conditionally to avoid recalling the witness presently on the stand at a later time.*

To an objection posed to extrinsic evidence; where the witness with the alleged bias, prejudice, interest, or improper motive has already testified:

- *I confronted this witness with (his) (her) (bias) (prejudice) (interest) (improper motive) during cross-examination when I asked (him) (her), and (he) (she) has not unequivocally admitted it.*

Cross-Reference to Texas Rule 613

Explanation

There is no rule that specifically deals with prejudice or improper motive. These are traditional types of impeachment that fall within the general impeachment provision of Rule 607.

A witness can be biased for as many reasons as there are for one person to be associated with another. A bias may be toward a party because of partiality, or against a party because of some animus or ill will.

—Impeachment— Character Evidence: Convictions and Specific Instances of Conduct

Objections

- *Objection. The conviction is neither for a felony nor is it a conviction for a crime involving moral turpitude.*
- *Objection. The probative value of the evidence on the issue of credibility does not outweigh its prejudicial effect. Specifically, probative value is low because:*

  (a) *the crime does not involve moral turpitude;* or

  (b) *though the crime involves moral turpitude, it is not very probative of untruthfulness because it does not involve any element of untruthfulness;* or

  (c) *the conviction, though less than ten years old, is still remote (and there have been no intervening convictions for a felony or a crime involving moral turpitude)*; or

(d) *credibility of this witness is not an important issue in this case because* ____ ______ (specifying reasons). *In addition, prejudice is high because* (specifically describing nature of prejudice, including any similarity between conduct involved in conviction and alleged conduct at issue in lawsuit).

- *Objection. This conviction is stale and inadmissible under Rule 609(b), because* (the date of the conviction) (the date of the witness's release from confinement) *occurred more than ten years ago and the probative value of the conviction on the issue of credibility does not substantially outweigh its prejudicial effect. Specifically, probative value is low because:*

  (a) the crime does not involve moral turpitude; or

  (b) *though the crime involves moral turpitude, it is not very probative of untruthfulness because it does not involve any element of untruthfulness;* or

  (c) *the conviction is remote (and there have been no intervening convictions for a felony or a crime involving moral turpitude);* or

I
J
K

(d) *credibility of this witness is not an important issue in this case because* __________ (specifying reasons)*;* or

(e) *prejudice is high because* (specifically describing nature of prejudice, including any similarity between conduct involved in conviction and alleged conduct at issue in lawsuit).

- *Objection. This conviction is inadmissible under Rule 609(c), because:*

  (a) *the witness (has been pardoned) (has had the conviction annulled) (has been given a certificate of rehabilitation), based upon a finding of rehabilitation, and there has been no subsequent conviction for a felony or a crime involving moral turpitude;* or

  (b) *the witness has lived out (his) (her) probation and has not subsequently been convicted of a felony or a crime involving moral turpitude;* or

  (c) *the witness (has been pardoned) (has had the conviction annulled), based upon a finding of innocence.*

- *Objection. The conviction is a juvenile adjudication which is inadmissible under Rule 609(d).*

- *Objection. The conviction is not final, because it is currently on appeal to the __________ court, and is therefore inadmissible under Rule 609(e).*
- *Objection. We have not received timely advance written notice of opponent's intent to use this conviction, despite our timely request for notice, and therefore it is inadmissible under Rule 609(f).*

To prior bad act evidence:

- *Objection. Specific instances of conduct are inadmissible to impeach under Rule 608(b).*

Responses

- *The witness was convicted of the* (felony offense of __________) (the offense of __________, a crime involving moral turpitude).

To an objection that probative value does not outweigh prejudicial effect:

- *The probative value of the conviction on the issue of credibility outweighs the prejudicial effect because:*

I
J
K

(a) *the offense is a felony;* or

(b*) the offense involves moral turpitude;* or

(c) *the offense was a premeditated and deliberate violation of the law, highly probative that the witness will likely disregard the oath; or*

(d) *the offense is not remote since it has only been* _______ (stating months/years) *since the date of (the conviction) (the witness's release from confinement);* or

I
J
K

(e) *there has been a subsequent conviction for the offense of (a felony) (a crime involving moral turpitude), and therefore any remoteness does not lower probative value;* or

(f) *credibility of this witness is important because* (explaining importance of witness's credibility).

If witness is a party:

- *The prejudice to the opposing party is minimal because the crime which is the subject of the conviction is dissimilar to the conduct at issue in this case.*

If witness is not a party:

- *The prejudice to the opposing party is minimal because the witness who was convicted is not a party.*

To an objection that the conviction is stale:

- *The probative value of the conviction on the issue of credibility substantially outweighs the prejudice to the opposing party because:*

  (a) *there has been a subsequent conviction for the offense of (a felony) (a crime involving moral turpitude), and therefore remoteness does not lower probative value;* or

  (b) *the offense is a felony;* or

  (c) *the offense involves moral turpitude;* or

  (d) *the offense was a premeditated and deliberate violation of the law, highly probative that the witness will likely disregard the oath;*

  (e) *the credibility of this witness is important because* (explaining importance of witness's credibility).

To an objection to a prior bad act:

- *This conduct of the witness is not offered to attack the witness's character for truthfulness but rather to:*

  (a) *show bias;*

  (b) *show interest;*

  (c) *show improper motive or influence;* or

  (d) *show a prior inconsistent statement;* or

  (e) *contradict the witness's direct examination testimony that* (fact to which witness testified that is inconsistent with prior bad act).

I
J
K

Cross-Reference to Texas Rules 608 and 609

Explanation

Rule 609(a) allows impeachment of a witness by showing conviction of a felony or a crime involving moral turpitude, regardless of punishment. The conviction is generally proved by testimony of the impeached witness or by documentary proof of the conviction. A judgment of conviction or a pen packet (certified public record from the prison) will suffice. Such proof must, of course, be authenticated. A certification under Rule 902(4) is the usual method of proof. If the witness does not admit the conviction, then proof must be made that the person convicted of the crime is the same person who is the witness. This proof may be made by fingerprint comparison by an expert, photographs, or by the testimony of a witness with knowledge.

An important issue concerns which offenses involve moral turpitude. There is no definition in the rules, and no satisfactory definition in the cases. The courts have held that moral turpitude includes more than crimes in the nature of crimen falsi, that is, crimes that involve some element of untruthfulness, deceit, or falsehood. In fact, moral turpitude includes some crimes of violence.

—Impeachment— Character Evidence: Opinion and Reputation

Objections

- *Objection. Counsel has failed to lay the proper predicate that the character witness has sufficient knowledge of the witness's character to give an opinion.*
- *Objection. Counsel has failed to lay the proper predicate that the character witness has sufficient knowledge of the witness's reputation to give an opinion concerning the nature of that reputation.*

In the guilt phase of a criminal trial:

- *Objection. Counsel has failed to lay the proper predicate that the character witness was familiar with the reputation prior to the day of the offense.*
- *Objection. Counsel has failed to lay the proper predicate that the character witness was familiar with the underlying facts or information upon which the opinion is based, prior to the day of the offense.*

To rehabilitative character testimony:

- *Objection. Counsel is bolstering the credibility of a witness whose character for truthfulness has not been attacked.*

Responses

- *A sufficient predicate has been laid to demonstrate the character witness's familiarity with* (the witness's character for truthfulness) *(the witness's reputation for truthfulness in the community) because* (explaining basis of knowledge).

I
J
K

To objection to rehabilitation:

- *The witness's character for truthfulness has been attacked because counsel attempted to impeach him by (opinion testimony) (reputation testimony) (conviction of a crime) (proof of improper motive or influence) (prior inconsistent statement) when the witness was cross-examined about* (explaining specifically the nature of the attack).

Cross-Reference to Texas Rules 404, 405, and 608

Explanation

A witness's credibility may be attacked by an extrinsic offer concerning the witness's character for truthfulness, that is, by the testimony of a character witness. The testimony of a character witness is limited in a number of ways. First, the character witness may testify only as to the character trait for truthfulness or untruthfulness of the principal witness (the witness being impeached). Second, the character witness is limited to testimony as to an opinion of the principal witness's character for truthfulness or untruthfulness, or testimony with regard to the witness's reputation for truthfulness or untruthfulness. The character witness may not testify to specific instances of conduct that form the basis of the opinion or reputation testimony. Third, in the guilt phase of a criminal trial, the state must prove as a preliminary fact that the character witness had knowledge of the defendant's character prior to commission of the crime in question.

—Impeachment— Contradiction

Objection

- *Objection. This is impeachment by extrinsic evidence on a collateral matter, because it concerns* (explaining with specificity why the matter is collateral).

Responses

- *The witness testified on direct examination that ______. This testimony is offered to impeach that testimony by contradiction.*
- *This is not impeachment on a collateral matter, because we would be entitled to prove (the contradicting fact) anyway because* (explaining the relevance of the fact independent of the contradiction).

Cross-Reference to Texas Rule 607

There are no rules specifically concerning impeachment by contradiction. This is a traditional method of impeachment that falls within the general impeachment provision of Rule 607.

I J K

Explanation

The question of relevance of the contradictory evidence would be decided under rules 401 and 402. Whether the matter is collateral is essentially an application of Rule 403—a collateral matter has low probative value and will necessarily cause undue delay

—Impeachment—
Perception or Memory

Objection

- *Objection. This is irrelevant because* (specifying why matter is irrelevant).

Responses

- *The question calls for an answer that will show the witness's inability to perceive. It is relevant to impeach the witness.*
- *The question calls for an answer that will show the witness's inability to remember the events about which (he) (she) has testified. It is relevant to impeach the witness.*

Cross-Reference to Texas Rule 607

No rule specifically deals with impeachment with regard to faulty perception or memory. This is a traditional method of impeachment that is governed by the relevance rules, as well as the general impeachment provision of Rule 607.

Explanation

Impeachment on the basis of faulty perception is a typical form of impeachment in cases that involve physical activity of the parties. Perception includes the ability to see, hear, smell, or feel something in question. Impeachment by showing faulty perception typically involves showing distraction on the part of the witness, physical impairment to perception, a state of excitement on the part of the witness that interferes with an ability to perceive, an obstruction to vision, or an impediment to hearing.

—Impeachment— Prior Inconsistent Statements

Objections

If offered without limitation:

- *Objection. The question calls for a hearsay statement.*

If offered for the purpose of impeachment:

- *Objection. The statement is not inconsistent with the witness's testimony and therefore is irrelevant to impeach.*

If admitted for the purpose of impeachment:

- *We request that the jury be instructed that it may not consider the statement for the truth of any fact stated, but only to determine the credibility of the witness.*

For failure to lay predicate as to a non-party witness:

- *Objection. Counsel has not laid the proper predicate, because the witness has not been advised of where, when, and to whom the statement was made.*
- *Objection. Counsel has not laid the proper predicate, because the witness has not been advised of the content of the statement.*

For impeachment by extrinsic evidence:

I
J
K

- *Objection. This is impeachment by extrinsic evidence on a collateral matter, because it concerns* (explaining with specificity why the matter is collateral).
- *Objection. Extrinsic evidence is inadmissible to impeach, because the witness was confronted with the statement and unequivocally admitted making it.*

Responses

To a relevance objection:

- *This statement is admissible to impeach. The witness testified on direct examination that _______, which is expressly inconsistent with this prior statement.*

To a hearsay objection:

- *This statement is not hearsay because:*

  (a) *under Rule 801(e)(1)(A), it is a prior statement of the witness given under oath, subject to the penalty of perjury, at a trial, hearing, or other proceeding, and is inconsistent with the witness's trial testimony;* or

  (b) *under Rule 801(e)(2), it is an admission of a party opponent;* or

  (c) *under Rule 801(e)(3), it was made in a deposition.*

- *This statement is admissible under the hearsay exception for* (stating specific exception).

- *This statement is admissible to impeach, and so is not hearsay. The witness testified on direct examination that ______, which is expressly inconsistent with this prior statement.*

I
J
K

If court sustains hearsay objection:

- *We offer this statement for the limited purpose of impeaching the witness with a prior inconsistent statement.*

To claimed lack of inconsistency:

- *This prior statement is inconsistent with the trial testimony because:*

  (a) *it omits a material detail which the trial testimony now includes;* or

  (b) *a prior statement of lack of memory is inconsistent with present recollection;* or

  (c) *the witness is obviously feigning present lack of memory.*

I J K

To predicate objection:

- *This prior inconsistent statement is an admission of a party opponent, and therefore, under Rule 613(a), the predicate of time, place, person, and content is not required.*
- *We are not required to show the witness his written statement prior to impeaching him under Rule 613(a).*

For impeachment by extrinsic evidence of a prior inconsistent statement:

- *The witness did not unequivocally admit making the prior inconsistent statement during cross-examination.*

- *This prior inconsistent statement is an admission of a party opponent, and therefore, under Rule 613(a), the predicate of time, place, person, and content is not required.*
- *This is not impeachment on a collateral matter, because we would be entitled to prove* (the fact contained in the statement) *anyway because* (explaining the relevance of the fact independent of the inconsistency).

Cross-Reference to Texas Rules 105, 613, 801, and 802

I
J
K

Explanation

Unless it falls under one of the exclusions of Rule 801(e), or an exception to the hearsay rule, the prior statement is not admissible for its truth. The statement would be admitted only for the fact that it was made—the limited purpose of impeachment. If requested, the objecting party is entitled, under Rule 105, to a limiting instruction. If admitted under an exclusion or an exception, the statement is admitted for its truth, rendering a limiting instruction inappropriate.

Texas requires a rigid predicate for impeachment by prior inconsistent statement as to any witness who does not fall under the admission of a party opponent rule. The witness must be told the contents of the statement, the time, place, and the person to whom it was made, and must be given an opportunity to explain or deny the statement.

Insurance Against Liability

Objection

- *May I approach the bench, Your Honor?* (At the bench) *Objection. The proponent is offering evidence of liability insurance on the issue of negligence or wrongful conduct in violation of Rule 411.*

Responses

- *This evidence of liability insurance is not offered on the issue of negligence, but to show (agency) (ownership) (control) (bias or prejudice of the witness).*
- *This evidence of liability insurance is not offered on the issue of negligence, but rather as net worth evidence to show what amount of punitive damages is sufficient to punish the defendant.*

I
J
K

Cross-Reference to Texas Rule 411

Explanation

Rule 411 forbids only the admission of proof of liability insurance on the issue of negligence or other wrongful conduct. Where evidence of liability insurance is offered for some other purpose, the rule does not bar its admission. For example, the rule mentions impeachment for bias as a relevant, non-negligence purpose.

Judicial Notice

Objection

- *I object to judicial notice of* (fact offered by opponent) *in that (it is not generally known in this jurisdiction) (it is open to dispute and not capable of ready and certain verification).*

Responses

- *Judicial notice of* (fact to be noticed*) is appropriate because (the fact is generally known by people in this jurisdiction, and to require other proof would waste the time of the court) (it is capable of ready and certain verification by resort to authoritative sources that have been provided to the court).*

Request for jury instruction

- *We request that the jury be instructed that it* (must) (may) *accept as conclusively proved the fact that* (specifying fact noticed).

Cross-Reference to Texas Rules 201–204

I
J
K

Explanation

Judicial notice is an effective and time-saving method of proving facts that are generally known in the jurisdiction or are capable of ready and certain verification by reference to authoritative sources. Judicial notice may be taken at any time during a proceeding, including at the appellate level. Rule 201 applies only to adjudicative facts, that is, facts that are in issue in the trial of a given case.

Judicially noticed facts are binding on the jury in civil cases. In criminal cases the jury may accept as true the judicially noticed fact, but is not required to. Under paragraph (g), if a judge in a criminal case takes judicial notice of a fact, the jury is not bound by that conclusion. The opposing party should request an instruction to that effect.

Rules 202–04 allow courts to take judicial notice of law, when appropriate. A court may take judicial notice of the law of other states, federal law, the law of other countries, municipal and county ordinances, the contents of the Texas Register, and agency rules. When parties disagree as to proper application of foreign law to the facts, the court is presented with a question of law and such a dispute will not preclude an otherwise proper motion for summary judgment. The party requesting such judicial notice must provide the court with authorities as to the substance of the law in question.

I
J
K

Lay Opinion Evidence

Objection

- *Objection. The question calls for a conclusion.*

Response

- *This is admissible as a lay opinion, under Rule 701, because it is rationally based on the perception of the witness and would help the jury to understand his testimony.*

Cross-Reference to Texas Rules 701 and 704

Explanation

Lay opinion is generally allowed where its admission makes the jury's fact-finding easier and more accurate, and where a witness provides an inference to the jury that takes the place of describing a series of perceptions which, in common experience, add up to a rather ordinary inference or characterization. In these situations, the lay person ordinarily describes his or her observations in terms of opinion. For example, witnesses will be allowed to testify that they observed a person who appeared happy, sad, nervous, excited, or depressed.

L
M
N

Leading Questions

Objection

- *Objection. The question is leading.*

Response

Usually no response is recommended. If, however, counsel desires to lead on direct examination, it may be necessary to respond in order to secure permission to do so.

- *We should be permitted to lead because:*

  (a) *it is necessary to develop the witness's testimony since the witness is having difficulty testifying because (he) (she) (is of tender years) (is impaired in giving testimony by reason of old age) (is of low intellect);* or

  (b) *the witness is (hostile) (an adverse party) (identified with an adverse party).*

Cross-Reference to Texas Rule 611(c)

Explanation

Rule 611(c) states that leading may be permitted on direct when it is necessary to develop the witness's testimony. Such situations typically involve an impairment in the ability of the witness to testify because of age, low intellect, or infirmity. On the other end of the spectrum, leading questions that explain technical testimony of an expert witness in terms understandable to laypersons will also typically be allowed. In addition, courts will usually permit leading on preliminary matters dealing with the witness's educational, occupational, or other noncontentious background matters. Leading may also be allowed to make transitions from one subject to another.

Misstating the Testimony

Objection

- *Objection. Counsel is misstating the testimony. The witness actually testified that ________.*

Response

- *The witness previously testified to ________.*

Cross-Reference to Texas Rule 611(a)

Explanation

This objection is sometimes available when the cross-examiner repeats the direct examination testimony of the witness being cross-examined (i.e., "you testified on direct that ________.") or refers to the previous testimony of another witness. The objection is designed to prevent counsel from shading the testimony of the witness as previously given.

Narratives

Objection

- *Objection. The question calls for a narrative.*

Response

None is recommended

Cross-Reference to Texas Rule 611(a)

Explanation

The orderly presentation of testimony requires that the examination proceed in question-and-answer form. Witnesses are not allowed to take the stand and testify to everything they know without benefit of questions. This objection seeks to assure objecting counsel of notice by the question as to objectionable testimony. When a witness testifies in a narrative form, the only available method of excluding objectionable testimony is by moving to strike after the testimony is given. While the motion to strike protects the record, it cannot strike the testimony from the minds of the jurors. In fact, the offending testimony may very well be cemented in the jurors' minds by the making of the motion to strike.

Non-Responsive Answers

Objection

- *Objection. The answer is non-responsive. The question asked for _______, and not ________.*

Response

Usually it is best not to respond, but rather to ask an additional question calling for the answer objected to.

Cross-Reference to Texas Rule 611(a)

Explanation

L M N

Questioning counsel has the right to require a witness to respond to legitimate questions. If a witness fails to respond to the question or exceeds the scope of the question, an objection and motion to strike the non-responsive portion of the question is permissible. Of course, control of the witness is the responsibility of questioning counsel. Tactically, questioning counsel may point out the failure of the witness to respond by repeating the same question, in exactly the same words, until the witness actually responds. This tactic not only elicits a response to the question, but also informs the jury that the witness is being evasive.

Objections Generally

Objections

- *Objection to (the question which calls for) (the witness's answer as to), because* (stating specific ground of objection).

If objection sustained as to prejudicial question or answer heard by jury:

- (Optional) *We move to strike the (question) (answer as to).*

If motion to strike granted:

- *We request that the jury be instructed to disregard.*

If jury instruction given:

- *We move for a mistrial.*

Running bill:

- *We request a running bill, or continuing objection, as to any testimony from (this witness) (any witness) concerning* (specific subject matter objected to) *on the basis that* (specifying ground of objection).

Response

- *The evidence is admissible because* (specifying theory of admission).

Cross-Reference to Texas Rule 103 and Texas Rules of Appellate Procedure 33.1, 44, 44.1, 44.2, 44.3, and 44.4

Explanation

The Texas Rules of Evidence require that counsel object to an offer of evidence in order to seek its exclusion. Thus, the court relies on counsel to call the inadmissibility of offered evidence to its attention. An appellate court will not review the erroneous admission of evidence to which no objection has been made unless, in a criminal case only, the error is fundamental.

O
P
Q

Objections must be timely in that they must be stated as soon as the objectionable nature of the question or answer becomes apparent. Thus, objections to the form of a question must be made at the time of the question. Similarly, when a question put to a witness calls for an inadmissible answer, the objection should be interposed before the answer. However, where the question on its face does not call for inadmissible evidence, but the witness's answer contains an inadmissible matter, then the objection is still considered timely if made immediately after the objectionable answer is given. A sustained objection must then be followed up by a request for a jury instruction and a motion for mistrial, as explained below.

An objection to an exhibit is usually timely if made when the exhibit is offered into evidence. However, if counsel or a witness attempts to disclose to the jury the content of any exhibit before it is offered, then the objection should be made when the disclosure is attempted. Occasionally, other rules or statutes may require pretrial objections. *See, e.g.*, Vernon's Ann. Texas Civ. Stat. art. 4590i, Sec. 14.01(e) (objections to expert qualifications in certain medical malpractice cases) Tex. R. Civ. P. 193.6 (objections to authenticity by party producing documents in discovery).

All objections must state the specific ground for excluding evidence unless the ground for the objection is obvious. It is not necessary that counsel state a rule number to be specific. The better practice is to state the nature of the rule violated with sufficient clarity that the court will understand which rule is being relied upon.

Offers of Proof

Forms of the Offer

Narrative offer of proof:

- *Your Honor, if allowed to answer this question the witness would testify to the following:* (stating substance of excluded testimony as well as any testimony needed to establish admissibility). *This evidence is admissible because* (stating grounds for the offer).

First question-and-answer method, if excluded testimony is short:

Ask each question, get the answer to that question, and then, after each answer, state the following:

- *We offer this question and answer as our (first) (second) (third) (. . .) offer of proof. May the record reflect that* (opposing party) *objected on the basis of* (ground of opponent's objection) *and that each such objection was sustained. We again request the court to allow its admission.* (Get ruling.) *This evidence is admissible because* (stating grounds for the offer). *That concludes our (first) (second) (third) (. . .) offer.*

Second question-and-answer method, if excluded testimony is extensive:

Ask all questions as if before the jury. At the conclusion of all excluded testimony state the following:

- *We tender each question and its answer separately and independently. May the record reflect that as to each question and its answer* (opposing party) *objected on the basis of* (ground of opponent's objection), *and that each such objection was sustained. We again request the court to allow admission of this evidence.* (Get ruling.) *This evidence is admissible because* (stating grounds for the offer). *That concludes our offer.*

Cross-Reference to Texas Rule 103 and Texas Rule of Appellate Procedure 33.1

Explanation

O
P
Q

When a question is posed to a witness at trial, and the court sustains an objection which precludes the witness's answer, the correctness of the court's ruling is difficult, if not in some cases impossible, to review on appeal unless the trial record contains the witness's proposed answer. Only then can the appellate court ascertain if the evidence, which would have been elicited but for the court's ruling, was truly inadmissible and if an erroneous exclusion was harmful error. The offer of proof supplies the witness's answer for the record. In the absence of the offer of proof, the appellate court may decline to review the trial court's ruling.

The offer of proof can be made in any of three ways, all outside the hearing of the jury. First, counsel may state in narrative form what the witness's testimony would have been. Second, counsel may submit a prepared, written narrative of the excluded testimony. Third, and the most common, counsel may question the witness to elicit the answers, as if testifying before the jury.

The offer of proof must be made before the charge is read to the jury or it will be waived

Payment of Medical and Similar Expenses

Objection

- *I object that this evidence is inadmissible as an offer to pay* (medical) (hospital) (repair) *expenses*

Response

- *This statement is admissible because it is not offered on the issue of liability, but rather to show* (specifying admissible purpose).

Cross-Reference to Texas Rule 409

Explanation

The rationale for this rule is similar to that of Rule 407 and Rule 408 relating to subsequent remedial measures and offers of compromise. The rule makers have excluded offers to pay medical expenses at trial so as to provide an incentive for those who believe themselves responsible, or those merely acting out of goodwill, to pay the expenses of victims without resort to the courts. When such bills are paid, the incentive to litigate is substantially lessened.

O
P
Q

—Privilege— Clergyman-Penintent Communication

Objection

- *Objection. The question calls for a communication protected by the clergy-penitent communication privilege.*

Response

- *The privilege is not applicable because:*

  (a) *the communication was not made in private;* or

  (b) *the communication was not intended to be confidential;* or

  (c) *the communication was made in the presence of ____________, a person whose presence did not further the purpose of the communication;* or

  (d) *the communication was made to ____________ in (his) (her) role as ____________, and not in (his) (her) role as a spiritual adviser.*

Cross-Reference to Texas Rule 505

Explanation

Confidential communications are privileged if they were made to a member of the clergy, or someone reasonably believed to be a member of the clergy. A member of the clergy is a functionary of a religious organization, such as a minister or rabbi.

The communication must be made privately and in confidence to a member of the clergy, who was acting in a professional capacity as a spiritual adviser. For example, marital counseling or counseling for other personal or emotional problems would certainly fall under the privilege.

—Privilege— Comment Upon Claim of Privilege

Objection

- *May I approach the bench Your Honor?* (At the bench) *Objection. Counsel has commented upon a privilege in violation of Rule 513(a).*

Response

- *Rule 513(c) permits comments upon claims of the privilege against self-incrimination by a party in the same proceeding.*

Cross-Reference to Texas Rule 513

Explanation

Rule 513(a) plainly expresses the proposition that invocation of a privilege may not be commented upon by judge or counsel, and no inferences may be drawn from it, even if it was claimed in a prior proceeding.

Rule 513(c) is an important exception to the protections outlined in Rules 513(a) and (b). A claim of the privilege against self-incrimination by a party in the same civil proceeding may be commented upon, adverse inferences may be drawn therefrom, and the party may be required to invoke it in front of the jury.

Either side in a criminal case (usually the state, but possibly a codefendant) may comment in final argument on the failure of the spouse to be called by the accused, if the other facts admitted in the case showed the spouse had knowledge of relevant facts.

—Privilege— Compelled Disclosure

Responses

- *The privilege has not been waived by voluntary disclosure because the disclosure was compelled erroneously by* (court ordering disclosure).
- *The privilege has not been waived by voluntary disclosure because the disclosure was made without opportunity for* (holder of privilege) *to claim the privilege.*

Cross-Reference to Texas Rule 512

Explanation

Rule 512 is a corollary to Rule 511. A compelled disclosure is not voluntary. Such a disclosure cannot be deemed a waiver by the holder of a privilege if the disclosure occurred because a court erroneously overruled the privilege claim.

Subsection (2) addresses the situation where the holder had no chance to claim the privilege. The effect of this rule is to remove any potential application of the old eavesdropper rule.

—Privilege— Husband-Wife Communication

Objections

- *Objection. The question calls for a communication protected by the husband-wife communication privilege.*
- *Objection.* (Name of spouse) *invokes the husband-wife testimonial privilege and declines to testify for the state.*

Responses

- *The communication privilege is not applicable because:*

  (a) *the communication was not made in private;* or

  (b) *the communication was not intended to be confidential;* or

  (c) *the communication was not intended to be confidential since reasonable precautions to protect confidentiality were not taken;* or

  (d) *the communication was made to aid commission of a crime or fraud, and so no privilege exists because of the exception contained in Rule 504(d)(1);* or

(e) *this is a proceeding brought by or on behalf of one spouse against the other spouse, and so no privilege exists because of the exception contained in Rule 504(d)(2)(A);* or

(f) *this is a proceeding between a surviving spouse and a person who claims through the deceased spouse, and so no privilege exists because of the exception contained in Rule 504(d)(2)(B);* or

(g) *this is a (commitment proceeding) (proceeding to place the spouse's person or property under the control of another because of the mental or physical condition of the spouse), and so no privilege exists because of the exception contained in Rule 504(d)(3);* or

(h) *this is a proceeding to establish the competence of a spouse, and so no privilege exists because of the exception contained in Rule 504(d)(4).*

- *The testimonial privilege is not applicable because:*

  (a) *the defendant's spouse wants to voluntarily testify.*

  (b) *only the spouse of an accused may invoke the privilege. The defendant may not invoke it.*

(c) *this is a proceeding in which the defendant is charged with a crime against (his or her spouse) (a member of the household) (a minor).*

(d) *the matters in question occurred prior to the marriage.*

Cross-Reference to Texas Rule 504

Explanation

Communications between husband and wife are protected in an attempt to respect confidences and protect the privacy of the marital relationship. However, the communication must be made to a spouse during the existence of a valid marriage, and invoked by the communicating spouse or someone on his or her behalf and there must be an intent to have a confidential communication. The privilege is held by the communicating spouse and continues after the termination of the marriage or the death of the communicating spouse.

In addition to the communication privilege, which applies in both civil and criminal cases, there is a testimonial privilege in criminal cases. This testimonial privilege prevents a spouse from being called to testify against an accused unless the alleged crime victim is the spouse, a member of either spouse's household, or any minor. If the event in question occurred prior to the marriage, the testimonial privilege does not apply.

O
P
Q

—Privilege—
Identity of Informer

Objection

- *Objection. The question calls for a matter protected by the privilege for the identity of informers.*

Responses

- *Invocation of this privilege should not be allowed because (the identity of the informer) (his interest in the subject matter of the communication) has already been disclosed to those who would have cause to resent the communication.*
- *Invocation of this privilege should not be allowed because the informer has appeared as a witness for the public entity holding the privilege.*
- *Invocation of this privilege should not be allowed because the informer is able to give testimony necessary to a fair determination of a material issue on the merits.*

Cross-Reference to Texas Rule 508

Explanation

Rule 508 offers state and federal law enforcement agents the opportunity to protect informers who assist them in investigations by granting a privilege to refuse to disclose their identity. Rule 508(b) provides that the privilege may be asserted by an appropriate representative of the public entity to which the information was furnished. The public entity holds this privilege, not the individual whose identity is at issue. The substance of any information given by the informer is not privileged, however, except as it may reveal the identity of the informer.

When it appears, either from the evidence or from some other showing by a party, that an informer may be able to give testimony as to a disputed issue of material fact, the court must make a determination as to whether the informer should be required to give such testimony. In criminal cases, the defendant has the burden to make a believable showing that the informer could give relevant testimony.

—Privilege—
Lawyer-Client Communication

Objection

- *Objection. The question calls for a confidential communication protected by the lawyer-client privilege.*

Response

- *The privilege is not applicable because:*

  (a) *the communication was not made for the purpose of facilitating the rendition of professional legal services;* or

  (b) *the communication was not intended to be confidential;* or

  (c) *the communication was not intended to be confidential since reasonable precautions to protect confidentiality were not taken;* or

  (d) *the communication was not between the lawyer and the client or client's representative since* (name of alleged client's representative) *was not a client's representative;* or

(e) *the legal services were sought or obtained to aid commission of a crime or fraud;* or

(f) *the communication relates to an issue between claimants through the same deceased client;* or

(g) *the communication relates to an issue of breach of duty between lawyer and client;* or

(h) *the communication relates to an issue concerning an attested document to which the lawyer is an attesting witness;* or

(i) *the communication relates to a matter of common interest between joint clients of the same lawyer.*

Cross-Reference to Texas Rule 503

Explanation

The heart of lawyer-client privilege is the requirement that the communication be confidential. This is a fact question of intent for the court to determine under Rule 104(a). The court will look to the circumstances to determine if the party intended that the communication not be disclosed to persons outside the relationship. An important subsidiary question is whether the party took any precautions to ensure confidentiality. The burden of proof is on the party claiming the privilege. This burden may be met by presenting evidence to the trial court in the form of live testimony, affidavits, depositions, and even by in-camera inspection of the documents themselves.

The communication must be made in connection with obtaining or rendering legal services, the mere fact that one party to the communication is an attorney is not sufficient to invoke the privilege. The privilege is not restricted to the client's communications. The lawyer's statements and advice are likewise protected.

Under Rule 503(b)(2), not only are communications to facilitate legal representation protected by attorney-client privilege in criminal cases, but also "any facts" which come to the lawyer because of the attorney-client relationship.

—Privilege—
Mental Health Information Communication

Objection

- *Objection. The question calls for a communication protected by the mental health information privilege.*

Response

- *The privilege does not apply because:*

  (a) *the communication was not made for purposes of diagnosis, evaluation, or treatment of a mental or emotional condition, alcoholism, or drug abuse;* or

  (b) *the communication was not intended to be confidential;* or

  (c) *the communication was not intended to be confidential since reasonable precautions to protect confidentiality were not taken;* or

  (d) *this is a proceeding brought by the patient against the professional, under the exception of Rule 510(d)(1);* or

(e) *the patient has consented to the release of medical information, under the exception of Rule 510(d)(2);* or

(f) *this is a proceeding brought by the professional against the patient to collect a fee, under the exception of Rule 510(d)(3);* or

(g) *the communication was made during a court-ordered examination after the patient was advised that such communications would not be privileged, under the exception of Rule 510(d)(4);* or

(h) *this is a proceeding in which* (party) *relies upon the (physical) (mental) (emotional) condition of* (name of patient) *as a part of a (claim) (defense) of* (specifying claim or defense), *under the exception of Rule 510(d)(5);* or

(i) *this is a proceeding regarding abuse or neglect of the resident of an institution, under the exception of Rule 510(d)(6).*

Cross-Reference to Texas Rule 510

Explanation

The rule attempts to protect privacy and encourage people to seek treatment, which often requires divulging private matters, by prohibiting disclosure in civil cases of communications to a professional. A consultation by a patient with a professional for the purposes of diagnosis, evaluation, or treatment of a mental or emotional condition protects all communications during that consultation. The privilege applies regardless of when the professional services were rendered, and continues to exist after the patient's death.

Because psychotherapy may involve discussion of all aspects of a patient's life, this privilege protects any confidential communication between patient and professional without regard to its substance. A communication is "confidential" under Rule 510(a)(4) if it is not intended to be disclosed to persons other than those present to further the interest of the patient, or reasonably necessary for the transmission of the communication, or who are participating in the diagnosis or treatment. The presence of nurses or the patient's family members does not destroy the privilege.

At the time of publication, case law permits ex parte communication between defense counsel and plaintiff's treating mental health professional.

—Privilege— Physician-Patient Communication

Objection

- *Objection. The question calls for a communication protected by the physician-patient privilege.*

Response

- *The privilege does not apply because:*

  (a) *the communication was not made relative to or in connection with the rendition of professional medical services;* or

  (b) *the communication was not intended to be confidential;* or

  (c) *the communication was not intended to be confidential since reasonable precautions to protect confidentiality were not taken;* or

  (d) *this is a proceeding brought by the patient against the physician, under the exception of Rule 509(e)(1);* or

(e) *the patient has consented to the release of medical information, under the exception of Rule 509(e)(2);* or

(f) *this is a proceeding brought by the physician against the patient to collect a fee, under the exception of Rule 509(e)(3);* or

(g) *this is a proceeding in which* (party) *relies upon the (physical) (mental) (emotional) condition of* (name of patient) *as a part of a (claim) (defense) of* (specifying claim or defense), *under the exception of Rule 509(e)(4);* or

(h) *this is a disciplinary proceeding against the (physician) (nurse), under the exception of Rule 509(e)(5);* or

(i) *this is a (proceeding for involuntary civil commitment) (proceeding for court ordered treatment) (probable cause hearing), under the exception of Rule 509(e)(6);* or

(j) *this is a proceeding regarding abuse or neglect of the resident of an institution, under the exception of Rule 509(e)(7).*

O
P
Q

Cross-Reference to Texas Rule 509

O
P
Q

Explanation

The physician-patient privilege protects confidential communications between a physician and a patient that relate to the professional services that the physician provides. The physician-patient relationship is contractual and wholly voluntary. It can be created by express or implied agreement. A single examination by medical personnel may create a sufficient relationship to allow the patient to invoke the privilege, even if the patient is unconscious at the time of treatment.

A communication is confidential if it is not intended to be divulged to persons other than those who are present to further the interest of the patient, reasonably necessary for the transmission of the communication, or working under the physician's care.

There is no physician-patient privilege in criminal cases except for communication by voluntary patients to anyone involved in treating or examining them for alcohol or drug abuse. Involuntary treatment or examination is not protected.

Rule 509

This rule governs disclosures of patient-physician communications only in judicial or administrative proceedings. Whether a physician may or must disclose such communications in other circumstances is governed by Tex. Rev. Civ. Stat. Ann. art. 4495b § 5.08 (now codified at Tex. Occ. Code Ann. ch. 159 (Vernon 2003)).

At the time of publication, case law permits ex parte communication between defense counsel and plaintiff's treating physician.

—Privilege— Political Vote

Objection

- *Objection. The question calls for a matter protected by the political vote privilege.*

Response

- *The privilege is not applicable because* (name of voter) *cast (his) (her) vote illegally.*

Cross-Reference to Texas Rule 506

Explanation

Because a secret ballot is a fundamental civil liberty essential to a democracy, voters are privileged from revealing how they cast their votes. The privilege only applies to legal voters, and a person who votes illegally may be compelled to disclose the candidates for whom the vote was illegally cast.

—Privilege—
Privileges Recognized Only as Provided

Cross-Reference to Texas Rule 501

Explanation

Rule 501 recognizes that unless there is some Constitutional provision, rule of evidence, statute, or valid court rule which renders the matter privileged, no one may lawfully refuse to disclose relevant evidence. The burden of establishing the applicability of a privilege is upon the party claiming a privilege, that is, the objecting party.

Statutory privileges include those for medical committees, Tex. Health & Safety Code Ann. Sec. 161.031–032 (Vernon Supp. 2003); medical peer review committees. Tex. Occ. Code Ann. Sec. 160.001–014 (Vernon 2003); dentists, *id.* Sec. 258.101–109; chiropractors, *id.* Sec. 201.401–405; and podiatrists, *id.* Sec. 201.401–407, 202.451–456.

The rules concerning privilege strike a balance between the potential damage to the relationship from disclosing the information and the benefit to be obtained from its disclosure. Rule 501 recognizes as a general proposition that all relevant evidence is discoverable. Rules 502–10 describe the privileges that render such evidence non-discoverable and inadmissible. Rules 511–13 deal with waiver, compulsion, and comment on the exercise of a privilege.

—Privilege— Required Reports

Objection

- *Objection. The question calls for a matter privileged by statute. Specifically,* (explaining nature and applicability of statutory privilege).

Response

- *The privilege is not applicable because:*

  (a) *the reporting party committed perjury in the report, so under the statute, the privilege does not arise;* or

  (b) *the reporting party made false statements in the report, so under the statute, the privilege does not arise;* or

  (c) *the reporting party committed fraud in the report, so under the statute, the privilege does not arise;* or

  (d) *other reasons privilege not applicable.*

Cross-Reference to Texas Rule 502

Explanation

Frequently, individuals or entities are required by law to provide governmental agencies with information that may be damaging if produced in a judicial proceeding. Compliance with the law may be hindered by the knowledge that the information could be used against the reporting party. To ensure accurate and complete reporting to agencies, therefore, many of the same laws provide that such information is privileged from disclosure and may not be disclosed by the agency receiving it. These reporting privileges may be created by Texas statutes or by statutes from other jurisdictions.

—Privilege— Trade Secrets

Objection

- *Objection. The question calls for a matter protected by the trade secret privilege.*

Responses

- *The privilege is not applicable because its effect would be to conceal fraud.*
- *The privilege should not bar disclosure because the interests of* (holder of trade secret) *can be adequately protected by confidentiality measures.*

Cross-Reference to Texas Rule 507

Explanation

A trade secret is a formula, pattern, device, or compilation of information which is used in one's business and which gives that person a competitive advantage. Disclosure of such information can harm the owner of the privilege by allowing competitors a window into his private business operations. Texas courts weigh the business interest of the holder of a trade secret against the need for full information in litigation and find a middle ground where both interests can be served.

An individual has the right to refuse to disclose a trade secret, if such withholding will not conceal fraud or otherwise work injustice. The rule specifically authorizes an employee or agent of the owner of the trade secret to claim the privilege as well.

A party seeking trade secret protection pursuant to Rule 507 must show (1) the extent to which the information is known outside of his business; (2) the extent to which it is known by employees and others involved in his business; (3) the extent of the measures taken by him to guard the secrecy of the information; (4) the value of the information; (5) the amount of effort or money expended by him in developing the information; and (6) the ease or difficulty with which the information could be properly acquired or duplicated by others.

—Privilege— Voluntary Disclosure

Responses

- *The privilege has been waived by voluntary disclosure of a significant part of the privileged matter under Rule 511(1) in that* (specifying nature and extent of disclosure); or
- *The privilege has been waived by consenting to disclosure of a significant part of the privileged matter under Rule 511(1) in that* (specifying nature and extent of consent to disclosure); or
- *The privilege has been waived, under Rule 511(2), by calling to testify as a character witness, when (he) (she) was a person to whom otherwise confidential communications were made.*

Cross-Reference to Texas Rule 511

Explanation

Rule 511 is a general waiver provision that applies to all of the privileges.

Generally, the party claiming a privilege has the burden of establishing the applicability of the privilege. The party seeking disclosure may oppose the privilege on the ground of waiver by voluntary disclosure. In civil cases, once it is proved that there has already been a disclosure of any significant part of the privileged matter the burden is upon the party asserting the privilege to prove that the disclosure did not constitute a waiver. In criminal cases the burden is on the party seeking the information to prove a waiver.

There is no clear standard as to when conduct will be held sufficient to imply waiver where there has been no express waiver. Implied waiver may exist as a result of partial disclosure of otherwise privileged matters.

Refreshing Present Recollection

Predicate to Refresh Recollection While Testifying

- *Can you presently remember* (factual matter to be refreshed)*?*
- *Would it refresh your memory if I showed you* (writing or other item used to refresh memory)*?*

Hand the writing or other item to the witness for examination.

- *Please read* (writing used to refresh memory) *to yourself.*
- *Have you read* (writing used to refresh memory)*?*
- *Do you now recall* _________ (factual matter to be refreshed)*?*
- *Tell the jury* _________ (factual matter to be refreshed).

Objections

- *Objection. This is an attempt to refresh the witness's recollection in the absence of a demonstrated failure of memory.*

R
S

- *Objection. The witness is reading from an exhibit which is not in evidence and is hearsay.*

Responses

- *The witness has shown a failure of memory, and I am attempting to refresh his recollection pursuant to Rule 612.*
- *The exhibit used to refresh the witness's recollection is already in evidence.*

Cross-Reference to Texas Rule 612

Explanation

A forgetful witness's memory may be refreshed by showing the witness an item, usually a writing, which jogs the witness's memory. This process can be helpful if the witness has a mental lapse or gets nervous on the stand. It permits the examiner to prompt the witness by the use of a document during the examination of the witness.

In civil cases, if the witness reviews a writing to refresh recollection *before testifying,* it is discretionary with the trial court whether to order production. In criminal

RS

cases, the court has no discretion and must order production, whether used before or during trial.

—Relevance— Generally

Objection

- *Objection. The question calls for an irrelevant answer because* (specifying why the subject is irrelevant).

Response

- *The evidence is relevant because* (specifying grounds of relevance).

Cross-Reference to Texas Rules 401 and 402

Explanation

Rule 401 defines "relevant evidence" as having any tendency to make the existence of any fact of consequence to the determination of the action more probable or less probable than it would be without the evidence. In other words, relevancy refers to the logical relationship between the proposed evidence and a fact to be established, that is, a tendency to establish a material proposition. The Rule 401 definition of relevance demonstrates the basic philosophy of the rules in favor

RS

of admitting evidence and allowing the fact-finder to determine the weight to be given the evidence. It is significant that the relevance rules only require that the evidence have some tendency to make the existence of a material fact more or less likely. There is no requirement that the tendency to make the existence of the fact more or less probable need be the most likely tendency or the best tendency.

Evidence offered to prove a proposition that has been stipulated does not render the evidence irrelevant although the proposition is no longer "in dispute." However, such evidence is subject to exclusion under Rule 403 since probative value of evidence offered to prove a stipulated issue is slight.

—Relevance— Conditional Admissibility

Objections

- *Objection. The evidence is not relevant because there has been no proof of* (specifying preliminary facts).
- *We move to strike the conditionally admitted evidence of ______. Counsel has failed to prove additional facts that are necessary to show the relevance of that conditionally admitted evidence.*

Responses

- *The relevance of this evidence has been shown through the testimony of* (name of witness), *who testified that* (specifying facts testified to).
- *We will show the relevance of this evidence by proof of* (specifying facts to be proved) *through the later testimony of* (name of witness), *and we ask the court to conditionally admit it at this time.*

Cross-Reference to Texas Rule 104

Explanation

Many rules of evidence require the proof of a preliminary fact, or the laying of a predicate, as a condition to admissibility of evidence. The most common preliminary fact questions governed by Rule 104(a) are hearsay predicates, privilege predicates, impeachment predicates, and opinion rule predicates.

The procedural rules are different when the relevance of the evidence depends upon proof of the preliminary facts. Such preliminary fact questions are decided under Rule 104(b) rather than Rule 104(a).

In making a determination on admissibility of evidence that depends for its relevance on the proof of other facts, the judge may conditionally admit the proffered evidence subject to later proof of the preliminary facts. This process is sometimes referred to as "connecting up." If the proponent fails to connect up or fulfill the terms of the conditional admission, a motion to strike the conditionally admitted evidence must be made.

—Relevance— Exclusion of Relevant Evidence on Special Grounds

Objections

Outside the hearing of the jury:

- *Objection. This evidence is inadmissible because its probative value is substantially outweighed by the danger of unfair prejudice. Probative value is low because:*

  (a) *the evidence is at most probative of a collateral rather than a central issue in the case;* or

  (b) *the proponent does not have a strong need for this evidence because* (stating reasons); or

  (c) *they have a less prejudicial way to prove* (proposition to be proved) *because they can prove* (specifying alternative means of proof); or

  (d) (proposition to be proved) *is not a disputed issue in the case. We have previously admitted* (proposition to be proved) *by our (pleadings) (answers to request for admissions)*; or

R
S

(e) *we offer to stipulate* (proposition to be proved); or

(f) *the logical inference from this evidence* (proposition to be proved) *is very weak because* (stating reasons); or

(g) *it requires stacking inference upon inference;* or

(h) *a reasonable jury could not infer* (proposition to be proved) *from this evidence;* or

(i) *the evidence is remote;* or

(j) *the evidence is very dissimilar to the incident in question.*

- *In addition, the danger of unfair prejudice is high because* (specifying nature of prejudice). *We object, then, because the danger of unfair prejudice substantially outweighs the very low probative value of this evidence.*

To evidence offered for a limited purpose:

- *Objection. This evidence is inadmissible because its probative value is substantially outweighed by the danger that the jury will be confused and misled to take the evidence for the inadmissible purpose,* (specifying inadmissible

R
S

purpose). *A limiting instruction would not be effective because* (explaining why limiting instruction would be ignored or ineffective). *This danger of jury confusion substantially outweighs the probative value since the evidence is offered only for the limited purpose of ________.*

In the hearing of the jury:

- *Objection. This evidence is inadmissible because its probative value is substantially outweighed by the cumulative nature of the evidence and the likelihood of undue delay as they needlessly take up the jury's time with unnecessary evidence. In addition, if* (opponent) *is allowed to go into this subject we will have no choice but to bring our own evidence on the point, delaying this trial even further. This unwarranted delay substantially outweighs what little probative value the evidence has.*

Responses

- *Counsel's objection goes to the weight rather than the admissibility of the evidence.*

R
S

- *Probative value is high because:*

  (a) *the evidence is corroborative of an issue central to the case;* or

  (b) *the evidence goes to the credibility of* (witness), *and (his) (her) testimony is important in this case;* or

  (c) *though this occurrence may be somewhat remote, there have been other intervening occurrences of the same nature which offset the effect of the remoteness. All of these occurrences should be seen by the jury together in order to get the full probative value of these occurrences;* or

  (d) *this evidence tends to prove* (admissible purpose) *which is directly in issue in the case.*

- *Any potential for (prejudice) (confusion of issues) is easily cured by an instruction.*

- *We agree that this evidence is prejudicial to* (party). *It's obvious that it very much hurts their case, but Rule 403 only calls for exclusion of unfairly prejudicial evidence. This evidence is not unfairly harmful to them because it does not cause the jury to decide the case on an improper basis. Rather, this evidence proves* (specify purpose), *which is a proper issue in the case.*

Cross-Reference to Texas Rule 403

Explanation

Although evidence may be logically relevant, that is, have probative value pursuant to Rule 401, it may still be excluded if its probative value is substantially outweighed by the collateral damage it causes in the trial. Rule 403 calls for a balancing by the court of probative value and the counter-factors listed in the rule. The balancing test is tilted heavily in favor of the admissibility of logically relevant evidence or evidence with probative value, in that the prejudice must substantially outweigh the probative value in order to warrant exclusion. Rule 403 balancing is appropriate to all offers of evidence, with the exception of offers under Rules 609(a), 609(b), and 705(d) which contain their own balancing tests.

The question of relevance of the contradictory evidence would be decided under rules 401 and 402. Whether the matter is collateral is essentially an application of Rule 403—a collateral matter has low probative value and will necessarily cause undue delay.

Offers to Stipulate

It is important to recognize that while a court does not have the authority to force a party to accept a stipulation, the power of the court to sustain a Rule 403 objection may effectuate such a result.

R S

—Relevance—
Limited Admissibility

Objections

- *Objection. This testimony is irrelevant to prove* (inadmissible purpose), *because* (specifying grounds of inadmissibility).
- *Objection. This testimony is irrelevant as to* (party against whom inadmissible), *because* (specifying grounds of inadmissibility).

To offer for limited purpose:

- *Objection. This evidence is inadmissible under Rule 403. Probative value is low because it is admissible only for the limited purpose of* (specify purpose) *against* (specify party) *only. This low probative value is substantially outweighed by the danger that the jury will be confused and misled to consider this as evidence of* (specifying inadmissible purpose) *against* (specifying party against whom inadmissible). *A limiting instruction would not be effective because* (specifying reasons for ineffectiveness).

Furthermore, there is a danger of unfair prejudice because (specifying nature of prejudice).

If initial objection overruled, or if sustained, but then admitted for limited purpose:

- *I request that the court instruct the jury that it may not consider this (testimony) (exhibit) as any evidence of* (inadmissible purpose) *against* (party against whom inadmissible), *but may only consider this evidence on the issue of* (admissible purpose) *against* (party against whom admissible).

Responses

- *This evidence is relevant and admissible for all purposes because* (specifying relevance).
- *This evidence is relevant and admissible against all parties because* (specifying relevance).

If objection sustained or court indicates intent to do so:

- *We offer* (specifying evidence) *for the limited purpose of proving* (specifying admissible purpose).
- *We offer* (specifying evidence) *only against* (specifying party against whom admissible) *and not against* (specifying party against whom inadmissible).

Cross-Reference to Texas Rule 105

Explanation

Rule 105 recognizes that evidence may be admissible for any number of purposes and allocates the responsibility to counsel to separate out the admissible from the inadmissible.

In cases involving multiple parties, the issue of limited admissibility arises when evidence is relevant and admissible against one party but not another. Once again, the burden is on the opponent to seek a limitation on the admission of evidence to appropriate parties by request for a limiting instruction.

Rule 105 operates in conjunction with Rule 103. Therefore, a proper objection under Rule 105 must be specific. The objecting party must clearly state the ground for his objection and specify with particularity what part of the evidence is objectionable. Furthermore, it is incumbent upon the opponent to seek limitation of the evidence to its proper admissible purpose, or against certain parties only, and to request a limiting instruction by the judge. Failure to do so results in admission of the evidence for all purposes and as to all parties.

—Relevance— Rule of Optional Completeness

Objection

- *At this time we invoke Rule 106 as to other portions of the (writing) (deposition) (recording) which are necessary to put in context this* (writing) *(deposition testimony) (recorded statement). We request that* (context completing statements) *be admitted at this time.*

Response

- *This (writing) (deposition testimony) (recorded statement) does not need explanation or context. The other parts are not necessary to a fair understanding of this evidence. If they want it in evidence they can offer it when they get the witness.*

Cross-Reference to Texas Rules 106 and 107

Explanation

R
S

The Rule of Optional Completeness is essentially a rule of fairness. It provides that the jury be given evidence of writings or statements in complete form when that complete form explains or gives context to the items being offered in evidence. The rule also applies to other writings or recorded statements that provide the same complete context in which the offered evidence should be considered. Rule 106 applies only to writings or recorded statements, while Rule 107 applies also to acts, declarations, and conversations.

R S

Repetitious Questions

Objection

- *Objection. The question is repetitious.*

Responses

- *The witness has not yet answered this particular question.*
- *The question has not been answered during my examination.*
- *This question is just a preface to a new line of questions.*

Explanation

For a court to sustain this objection, a precise question must have been asked, and a response given during the examination of questioning counsel. The objection, therefore, will not lie where, on cross-examination, counsel asks for testimony elicited earlier during direct examination. A court may sustain the objection when on redirect examination a question is asked that was already answered during direct examination. The objection also applies when a witness is recalled to testify. Of course,

R S

whether such an objection is sustained is strictly within the discretion of the trial judge.

Subsequent Remedial Measures

Objections

- *Objection. This is evidence of a subsequent remedial measure, inadmissible under Rule 407 to prove negligence or culpable conduct.*

To offer of subsequent measure for a limited purpose:

- *Objection. We offer to stipulate (ownership) (control) (feasibility of precautionary measures). Since this issue is not controverted, the subsequent measure is inadmissible under Rule 407, and it is also immaterial.*
- *Objection. In addition to our objection under Rule 407, we object under Rule 403 to admission for the purpose stated by counsel. Probative value is low because it is admissible only for that limited purpose. This low probative value is substantially outweighed by the danger that the jury will be confused and misled to consider this as evidence of*

R
S

negligence. A limiting instruction would not be effective because (specifying reasons for ineffectiveness). *Furthermore, there is a danger of unfair prejudice because* (specifying nature of prejudice).

If a Rule 407 objection is overruled, or if sustained, but then admitted for limited purpose:

- *I request that the court instruct the jury that it may not consider this (testimony) (exhibit) as any evidence of negligence or culpable conduct, but may only consider this evidence on the issue of* (admissible purpose).

Response

- *This evidence is not offered on the issue of negligence or culpable conduct, but is offered:*

  (a) *to show ownership of* (explaining relevance to show ownership); or

  (b) *to show control of* (explaining relevance to show control); *to show feasibility of precautionary measures in that* (explaining relevance to show feasibility)*; to impeach* (name of witness) *whose testimony was contradicted by subsequent remedial measure; or on the*

RS

strict liability count to show that the product is unreasonably dangerous.

Cross-Reference to Texas Rule 407

Explanation

Evidence of subsequent remedial measures is per se inadmissible on the issues of negligence or culpable conduct only. The reason for such evidentiary bar is to remove any disincentive to correct defective conditions.

Unlike Rule 407 of the Federal Rules of Evidence, subsequent remedial measures are not excluded by the Texas rule if offered to prove strict liability. In addition, under the Texas rule, Rule 407(b), a written notification by a manufacturer to a purchaser, of defect in a product may be admissible against the manufacturer, if relevant to show the defect.

The evidentiary bar of Rule 407 is limited to the exclusion of remedial measures when offered on an issue of negligence or culpable conduct. The rule explicitly allows the offer of a subsequent remedial measure for any other relevant purpose, including but not limited to, ownership or control of the repaired property, and the feasibility of precautionary measures, if controverted.

RS

Texas Rules of Evidence

Texas Rules of Evidence

Effective January 1, 1999

Contents

ARTICLE III PRESUMPTIONS

[No rules adopted at this time}

ARTICLE IV RELEVANCY AND ITS LIMITS

ARTICLE V PRIVILEGES

ARTICLE VI WITNESSES

ARTICLE VIII HEARSAY

ARTICLE IX AUTHENTICATION AND IDENTIFICATION

ARTICLE X CONTENTS OF WRITINGS, RECORDINGS, AND PHOTOGRAPHS

Texas Rules of Evidence
Effective January 1, 1999

ARTICLE I. GENERAL PROVISIONS

RULE 101. TITLE AND SCOPE

(a) Title. These rules shall be known and cited as the Texas Rules of Evidence.

(b) Scope. Except as otherwise provided by statute, these rules govern civil and criminal proceedings (including examining trials before magistrates) in all courts of Texas, except small claims courts.

(c) Hierarchical Governance in Criminal Proceedings. Hierarchical governance shall be in the following order: the Constitution of the United States, those federal statutes that control states under the supremacy clause, the Constitution of Texas, the Code of Criminal Procedure and the Penal Code, civil statutes, these rules, and the common law. Where possible, inconsistency is to be removed by reasonable construction.

(d) Special Rules of Applicability in Criminal Proceedings.

(1) Rules not applicable in certain proceedings. These rules, except with respect to privileges, do not apply in the following situations:

(A) the determination of questions of fact preliminary to admissibility of evidence when the issue is to be determined by the court under Rule 104;

(B) proceedings before grand juries;

(C) proceedings in an application for habeas corpus in extradition, rendition, or interstate detainer;

(D) a hearing under Code of Criminal Procedure article 46.02, by the court out of the presence of a jury, to determine whether there is sufficient evidence of incompetency to require a jury determination of the question of incompetency;

(E) proceedings regarding bail except hearings to deny, revoke or increase bail;

(F) a hearing on justification for pretrial detention not involving bail;

(G) proceedings for the issuance of a search or arrest warrant; or

(H) proceedings in a direct contempt determination.

(2) Applicability of privileges. These rules with respect to privileges apply at all stages of all actions, cases, and proceedings.

(3) Military justice hearings. Evidence in hearings under the Texas Code of Military Justice, Tex. Gov't Code §432.001-432.195, shall be governed by that Code.

RULE 102. PURPOSE AND CONSTRUCTION

These rules shall be construed to secure fairness in administration, elimination of unjustifiable expense and delay, and promotion of growth and development of the law of evidence to the end that the truth may be ascertained and proceedings justly determined.

RULE 103. RULINGS ON EVIDENCE

(a) Effect of Erroneous Ruling. Error may not be predicated upon a ruling which admits or excludes evidence unless a substantial right of the party is affected, and

(1) Objection. In case the ruling is one admitting evidence, a timely objection or motion to strike appears of record, stating the specific ground of objection, if the specific ground was not apparent from the context. When the court hears objections to offered evidence out of the presence of the jury and rules that such evidence be admitted, such objections shall be deemed to apply to such evidence when it is admitted before the jury without the necessity of repeating those objections.

(2) Offer of proof. In case the ruling is one excluding evidence, the substance of the evidence was made known to the court by offer, or was apparent from the context within which questions were asked.

(b) Record of Offer and Ruling. The offering party shall, as soon as practicable, but before the court's charge is read to the jury, be allowed to make, in the absence of the jury, its offer of proof. The court may add any other or further statement which shows the character of the evidence, the form in which it was offered, the objection made, and the ruling thereon. The court may, or at the request of a party shall, direct the making of an offer in question and answer form.

(c) Hearing of Jury. In jury cases, proceedings shall be conducted, to the extent practicable, so as to prevent inadmissible evidence from being suggested to the jury by any means, such as making statements or offers of proof or asking questions in the hearing of the jury.

(d) Fundamental Error in Criminal Cases. In a criminal case, nothing in these rules precludes taking notice of fundamental errors affecting substantial rights although they were not brought to the attention of the court.

RULE 104. PRELIMINARY QUESTIONS

(a) Questions of Admissibility Generally. Preliminary questions concerning the qualification of a person to be a witness, the existence of a privilege, or the admissibility of evidence shall be determined by the court, subject to the provisions of subdivision (b). In making its determination the court is not bound by the rules of evidence except those with respect to privileges.

(b) Relevancy Conditioned on Fact. When the relevancy of evidence depends upon the fulfillment of a condition of fact, the court shall admit it upon, or subject to, the introduction of evidence sufficient to support a finding of the fulfillment of the condition.

(c) Hearing of Jury. In a criminal case, a hearing on the admissibility of a confession shall be conducted out of the hearing of the jury. All other civil or criminal hearings on preliminary matters shall be conducted out of the hearing of the jury when the interests of justice so require or in a criminal case when an accused is a witness and so requests.

(d) Testimony by Accused Out of the Hearing of the Jury. The accused in a criminal case does not, by testifying upon a preliminary matter out of the hearing of the jury, become subject to cross-examination as to other issues in the case.

(e) Weight and Credibility. This rule does not limit the right of a party to introduce before the jury evidence relevant to weight or credibility.

RULE 105. LIMITED ADMISSIBILITY

(a) Limiting Instruction. When evidence which is admissible as to one party or for one purpose but not admissible as to another party or for another purpose is admitted, the court, upon request, shall restrict the evidence to its proper scope and instruct the jury accordingly; but, in the absence of such request the court's action in admitting such evidence without limitation shall not be a ground for complaint on appeal.

(b) Offering Evidence for Limited Purpose. When evidence referred to in paragraph (a) is excluded, such exclusion shall not be a ground for complaint on appeal unless the proponent expressly offers the evidence for its limited, admissible purpose or limits its offer to the party against whom it is admissible.

RULE 106. REMAINDER OF OR RELATED WRITINGS OR RECORDED STATEMENTS

When a writing or recorded statement or part thereof is introduced by a party, an adverse party may at that time introduce any other part or any other writing or recorded statement which ought in fairness to be considered contemporaneously with it. "Writing or recorded statement" includes depositions.

RULE 107. RULE OF OPTIONAL COMPLETENESS

When part of an act, declaration, conversation, writing or recorded statement is given in evidence by one party, the whole on the same subject may be inquired into by the other, and any other act, declaration, writing or recorded statement which is necessary to make it fully understood or to explain the same may also be given in evidence, as when a letter is read, all letters on the same subject between the same parties may be given. "Writing or recorded statement" includes depositions.

ARTICLE II. JUDICIAL NOTICE

RULE 201. JUDICIAL NOTICE OF ADJUDICATIVE FACTS

(a) Scope of Rule. This rule governs only judicial notice of adjudicative facts.

(b) Kinds of Facts. A judicially noticed fact must be one not subject to reasonable dispute in that it is either (1) generally known within the territorial jurisdiction of the trial court or (2) capable of accurate and ready determination by resort to sources whose accuracy cannot reasonably be questioned.

(c) When Discretionary. A court may take judicial notice, whether requested or not.

(d) When Mandatory. A court shall take judicial notice if requested by a party and supplied with the necessary information.

(e) Opportunity to Be Heard. A party is entitled upon timely request to an opportunity to be heard as to the propriety of taking judicial notice and the tenor of the matter noticed. In the absence of prior notification, the request may be made after judicial notice has been taken.

(f) Time of Taking Notice. Judicial notice may be taken at any stage of the proceeding.

(g) Instructing Jury. In civil cases, the court shall instruct the jury to accept as conclusive any fact judicially noticed. In criminal cases, the court shall instruct the jury that it may, but is not required to, accept as conclusive any fact judicially noticed.

RULE 202. DETERMINATION OF LAW OF OTHER STATES

A court upon its own motion may, or upon the motion of a party shall, take judicial notice of the constitutions, public statutes, rules, regulations, ordinances, court decisions, and common law of every other state, territory, or jurisdiction of the United States. A party requesting that judicial notice be taken of such matter shall furnish the court sufficient information to enable it properly to comply with the request, and shall give all parties such notice, if any, as the court may deem necessary, to enable all parties fairly to prepare to meet the request. A party is entitled upon timely request to an opportunity to be heard as to the propriety of taking judicial notice and the tenor of the matter noticed. In the absence of prior notification, the request may be made after judicial notice has been taken. Judicial notice of such matters may be taken at any stage of the proceeding. The court's determination shall be subject to review as a ruling on a question of law.

RULE 203. DETERMINATION OF THE LAWS OF FOREIGN COUNTRIES

A party who intends to raise an issue concerning the law of a foreign country shall give notice in the pleadings or other reasonable written notice, and at least 30 days prior to the date of trial such party shall furnish all parties copies of any written materials or sources that the party intends to use as proof of the foreign law. If the materials or sources were originally written in a language other than English, the party intending to rely upon them shall furnish all parties both a copy of the foreign language text and an English translation. The court, in determining the law of a foreign nation, may consider any material or source, whether or not submitted by a party or admissible under the rules of evidence, including but not limited to affidavits, testimony, briefs, and treatises. If the court considers sources other than those submitted by a party, it shall give all parties notice and a reasonable opportunity to comment on the sources and to submit further materials for review by the court. The court, and not a jury, shall determine the laws of foreign countries. The court's determination shall be subject to review as a ruling on a question of law.

RULE 204. DETERMINATION OF TEXAS CITY AND COUNTY ORDINANCES, THE CONTENTS OF THE TEXAS REGISTER, AND THE RULES OF AGENCIES PUBLISHED IN THE ADMINISTRATIVE CODE

A court upon its own motion may, or upon the motion of a party shall, take judicial notice of the ordinances of municipalities and counties of Texas, of the contents of the Texas Register, and of the codified rules of the agencies published in the Administrative Code. Any party requesting that judicial notice be taken of such matter shall furnish the court sufficient information to enable it properly to comply with the request, and shall give all parties such notice, if any, as the court may deem necessary, to enable all parties fairly to prepare to meet the request. A party is entitled upon timely request to an opportunity to be heard as to the propriety of taking judicial notice and the tenor of the matter noticed. In the absence of prior notification, the request may be made after judicial notice has been taken. The court's determination shall be subject to review as a ruling on a question of law.

ARTICLE III. PRESUMPTIONS

[No rules adopted at this time.]

ARTICLE IV. RELEVANCY AND ITS LIMITS

RULE 401. DEFINITION OF "RELEVANT EVIDENCE"

"Relevant evidence" means evidence having any tendency to make the existence of any fact that is of consequence to the determination of the action more probable or less probable than it would be without the evidence.

RULE 402. RELEVANT EVIDENCE GENERALLY ADMISSIBLE; IRRELEVANT EVIDENCE INADMISSIBLE

All relevant evidence is admissible, except as otherwise provided by Constitution, by statute, by these rules, or by other rules prescribed pursuant to statutory authority. Evidence which is not relevant is inadmissible.

RULE 403. EXCLUSION OF RELEVANT EVIDENCE ON SPECIAL GROUNDS

Although relevant, evidence may be excluded if its probative value is substantially outweighed by the danger of unfair prejudice, confusion of the issues, or misleading the jury, or by considerations of undue delay, or needless presentation of cumulative evidence.

RULE 404. CHARACTER EVIDENCE NOT ADMISSIBLE TO PROVE CONDUCT; EXCEPTIONS; OTHER CRIMES

(a) Character Evidence Generally. Evidence of a person's character or character trait is not admissible for the purpose of proving action in conformity therewith on a particular occasion, except:

(1) Character of accused. Evidence of a pertinent character trait offered:

(A) by an accused in a criminal case, or by the prosecution to rebut the same, or

(B) by a party accused in a civil case of conduct involving moral turpitude, or by the accusing party to rebut the same;

(2) Character of victim. In a criminal case and subject to Rule 412, evidence of a pertinent character trait of the victim of the crime offered by an accused, or by the prosecution to rebut the same, or evidence of peaceable character of the victim offered by the prosecution in a homicide case to rebut evidence that the victim was the first aggressor; or in a civil case, evidence of character for violence of the alleged victim of assaultive conduct offered on the issue of self-defense by a party accused of the assaultive conduct, or evidence of peaceable character to rebut the same;

(3) Character of witness. Evidence of the character of a witness, as provided in rules 607, 608 and 609.

(b) Other Crimes, Wrongs or Acts. Evidence of other crimes, wrongs or acts is not admissible to prove the character of a person in order to show action in conformity therewith. It may, however, be admissible for other purposes, such as proof of motive, opportunity, intent, preparation, plan, knowledge, identity, or absence of mistake or accident, provided that upon timely request by the accused in a criminal case, reasonable notice is given in advance of trial of intent to introduce in the State's case-in-chief such evidence other than that arising in the same transaction.

RULE 405. METHODS OF PROVING CHARACTER

(a) Reputation or Opinion. In all cases in which evidence of a person's character or character trait is admissible, proof may be made by testimony as to reputation or by testimony in the form of an opinion. In a criminal case, to be qualified to testify at the guilt stage of trial concerning the character or character trait of an accused, a witness must have been familiar with the reputation, or with the underlying facts or information upon which the opinion is based, prior to the day of the offense. In all cases where testimony is admitted under this rule, on cross-examination inquiry is allowable into relevant specific instances of conduct.

(b) Specific Instances of Conduct. In cases in which a person's character or character trait is an essential element of a charge, claim or defense, proof may also be made of specific instances of that person's conduct.

RULE 406. HABIT; ROUTINE PRACTICE

Evidence of the habit of a person or of the routine practice of an organization, whether corroborated or not and regardless of the presence of eyewitnesses, is relevant to prove that the conduct of the person or organization on a particular occasion was in conformity with the habit or routine practice.

RULE 407. SUBSEQUENT REMEDIAL MEASURES; NOTIFICATION OF DEFECT

(a) Subsequent Remedial Measures. When, after an event, measures are taken which, if taken previously, would have made the event less likely to occur, evidence of the subsequent remedial measures is not admissible to prove negligence or culpable conduct in connection with the event. This rule does not require the exclusion of evidence of subsequent remedial measures when offered for another purpose, such as proving ownership, control or feasibility of precautionary measures, if controverted, or impeachment. Nothing in this rule shall preclude admissibility in products liability cases based on strict liability.

(b) Notification of Defect. A written notification by a manufacturer of any defect in a product produced by such manufacturer to purchasers thereof is admissible against the manufacturer on the issue of existence of the defect to the extent that it is relevant.

RULE 408. COMPROMISE AND OFFERS TO COMPROMISE

Evidence of (1) furnishing or offering or promising to furnish or (2) accepting or offering or promising to accept, a valuable consideration in compromising or attempting to compromise a claim which was disputed as to either validity or amount is not admissible to prove liability for or invalidity of the claim or its amount. Evidence of conduct or statements made in compromise negotiations is likewise not admissible. This rule does not require the exclusion of any evidence otherwise discoverable merely because it is presented in the course of compromise negotiations. This rule also does not require exclusion when the evidence is offered for another purpose, such as proving bias or prejudice or interest of a witness or a party, negativing a contention of undue delay, or proving an effort to obstruct a criminal investigation or prosecution.

RULE 409. PAYMENT OF MEDICAL AND SIMILAR EXPENSES

Evidence of furnishing or offering or promising to pay medical, hospital, or similar expenses occasioned by an injury is not admissible to prove liability for the injury.

RULE 410. INADMISSIBILITY OF PLEAS, PLEA DISCUSSIONS AND RELATED STATEMENTS

Except as otherwise provided in this rule, evidence of the following is not admissible against the defendant who made the plea or was a participant in the plea discussions:

(1) a plea of guilty that was later withdrawn;

(2) in civil cases, a plea of nolo contendere, and in criminal cases, a plea of nolo contendere that was later withdrawn;

(3) any statement made in the course of any proceedings under Rule 11 of the Federal Rules of Criminal Procedure or comparable state procedure regarding, in a civil case, either a plea of guilty that was later withdrawn or a plea of nolo contendere, or in a criminal case, either a plea of guilty that was later withdrawn or a plea of nolo contendere that was later withdrawn; or

(4) any statement made in the course of plea discussions with an attorney for the prosecuting authority, in a civil case, that do not result in a plea of guilty or that result in a plea of guilty later withdrawn, or in a criminal case, that do not result in a plea of guilty or a plea of nolo contendere or that results in a plea, later withdrawn, of guilty or nolo contendere.

However, such a statement is admissible in any proceeding wherein another statement made in the course of the same plea or plea discussions has been introduced and the statement ought in fairness be considered contemporaneously with it.

RULE 411. LIABILITY INSURANCE

Evidence that a person was or was not insured against liability is not admissible upon the issue whether the person acted negligently or otherwise wrongfully. This rule does not require the exclusion of evidence of insurance against liability when offered for another issue, such as proof of agency, ownership, or control, if disputed, or bias or prejudice of a witness.

RULE 412. EVIDENCE OF PREVIOUS SEXUAL CONDUCT IN CRIMINAL CASES

(a) Reputation or Opinion Evidence. In a prosecution for sexual assault or aggravated sexual assault, or attempt to commit sexual assault or aggravated sexual assault, reputation or opinion evidence of the past sexual behavior of an alleged victim of such crime is not admissible.

(b) Evidence of Specific Instances. In a prosecution for sexual assault or aggravated sexual assault, or attempt to commit sexual assault or aggravated sexual assault, evidence of specific instances of an alleged victim's past sexual behavior is also not admissible, unless:

(1) such evidence is admitted in accordance with paragraphs (c) and (d) of this rule;

(2) it is evidence:

(A) that is necessary to rebut or explain scientific or medical evidence offered by the State;

(B) of past sexual behavior with the accused and is offered by the accused upon the issue of whether the alleged victim consented to the sexual behavior which is the basis of the offense charged;

(C) that relates to the motive or bias of the alleged victim;

(D) is admissible under Rule 609; or

(E) that is constitutionally required to be admitted; and

(3) its probative value outweighs the danger of unfair prejudice.

(c) Procedure for Offering Evidence. If the defendant proposes to introduce any documentary evidence or to ask any question, either by direct examination or cross-examination of any witness, concerning specific instances of the alleged victim's past sexual behavior, the defendant must inform the court out of the hearing of the jury prior to introducing any such evidence or asking any such question. After this notice, the court shall conduct an in camera hearing, recorded by the court reporter, to determine whether the proposed evidence is admissible under paragraph (b) of this rule. The court shall determine what evidence is admissible and shall accordingly limit the questioning. The defendant shall not go outside these limits or refer to any evidence ruled inadmissible in camera without prior approval of the court without the presence of the jury.

(d) Record Sealed. The court shall seal the record of the in camera hearing required in paragraph (c) of this rule for delivery to the appellate court in the event of an appeal.

(e) Sexual Conduct of Child as Defense. This rule does not limit the right of the accused to produce evidence of promiscuous sexual conduct of a child 14 years old or older as a defense to sexual assault, aggravated sexual assault, indecency with a child or an attempt to commit any of the foregoing crimes. If such evidence is admitted, the court shall instruct the jury as to the purpose of the evidence and as to its limited use.

ARTICLE V. PRIVILEGES

RULE 501. PRIVILEGES RECOGNIZED ONLY AS PROVIDED

Except as otherwise provided by Constitution, by statute, by these rules, or by other rules prescribed pursuant to statutory authority, no person has a privilege to:

(1) refuse to be a witness;

(2) refuse to disclose any matter;

(3) refuse to produce any object or writing; or

(4) prevent another from being a witness or disclosing any matter or producing any object or writing.

RULE 502. REQUIRED REPORTS PRIVILEGED BY STATUTE

A person, corporation, association, or other organization or entity, either public or private, making a return or report required by law to be made has a privilege to refuse to disclose and to prevent any other person from disclosing the return or report, if the law requiring it to be made so provides. A public officer or agency to whom a return or report is required by law to be made has a privilege to refuse to disclose the return or report if the law requiring it to be made so provides. No privilege exists under this rule in actions involving perjury, false statements, fraud in the return or report, or other failure to comply with the law in question.

RULE 503. LAWYER-CLIENT PRIVILEGE

(a) Definitions. As used in this rule:

(1) A "client" is a person, public officer, or corporation, association, or other organization or entity, either public or private, who is rendered professional legal services by a lawyer, or who consults a lawyer with a view to obtaining professional legal services from that lawyer.

(2) A "representative of the client" is:

(A) a person having authority to obtain professional legal services, or to act on advice thereby rendered, on behalf of the client, or

(B) any other person who, for the purpose of effectuating legal representation for the client, makes or receives a confidential communication while acting in the scope of employment for the client.

(3) A "lawyer" is a person authorized, or reasonably believed by the client to be authorized, to engage in the practice of law in any state or nation.

(4) A "representative of the lawyer" is:

(A) one employed by the lawyer to assist the lawyer in the rendition of professional legal services; or

(B) an accountant who is reasonably necessary for the lawyer's rendition of professional legal services.

(5) A communication is "confidential" if not intended to be disclosed to third persons other than those to whom disclosure is made in furtherance of the rendition of professional legal services to the client or those reasonably necessary for the transmission of the communication.

(b) Rules of Privilege.

(1) General rule of privilege. A client has a privilege to refuse to disclose and to prevent any other person from disclosing confidential communications made for the purpose of facilitating the rendition of professional legal services to the client:

(A) between the client or a representative of the client and the client's lawyer or a representative of the lawyer;

(B) between the lawyer and the lawyer's representative;

(C) by the client or a representative of the client, or the client's lawyer or a representative of the lawyer, to a lawyer or a representative of a lawyer representing another party in a pending action and concerning a matter of common interest therein;

(D) between representatives of the client or between the client and a representative of the client; or

(E) among lawyers and their representatives representing the same client.

(2) Special rule of privilege in criminal cases. In criminal cases, a client has a privilege to prevent the lawyer or lawyer's representative from disclosing any other fact which came to the knowledge of the lawyer or the lawyer's representative by reason of the attorney-client relationship.

(c) Who May Claim the Privilege. The privilege may be claimed by the client, the client's guardian or conservator, the personal representative of a deceased client, or the successor, trustee, or similar representative of a corporation, association, or other organization, whether or not in existence. The person who was the lawyer or the lawyer's representative at the time of the communication is presumed to have authority to claim the privilege but only on behalf of the client.

(d) Exceptions. There is no privilege under this rule:

(1) Furtherance of crime or fraud. If the services of the lawyer were sought or obtained to enable or aid anyone to commit or plan to commit what the client knew or reasonably should have known to be a crime or fraud;

(2) Claimants through same deceased client. As to a communication relevant to an issue between parties who claim through the same deceased client, regardless of whether the claims are by testate or intestate succession or by inter vivos transactions;

(3) Breach of duty by a lawyer or client. As to a communication relevant to an issue of breach of duty by a lawyer to the client or by a client to the lawyer;

(4) Document attested by a lawyer. As to a communication relevant to an issue concerning an attested document to which the lawyer is an attesting witness; or

(5) Joint clients. As to a communication relevant to a matter of common interest between or among two or more clients if the communication was made by any of them to a lawyer retained or consulted in common, when offered in an action between or among any of the clients.

RULE 504. HUSBAND-WIFE PRIVILEGES

(a) Confidential Communication Privilege.

(1) Definition. A communication is confidential if it is made privately by any person to the person's spouse and it is not intended for disclosure to any other person.

(2) Rule of privilege. A person, whether or not a party, or the guardian or representative of an incompetent or deceased person, has a privilege during marriage and afterwards to refuse to disclose and to prevent another from disclosing a confidential communication made to the person's spouse while they were married.

(3) Who may claim the privilege. The confidential communication privilege may be claimed by the person or the person's guardian or representative, or by the spouse on the person's behalf. The authority of the spouse to do so is presumed.

(4) Exceptions. There is no confidential communication privilege:

(A) **Furtherance of Crime or Fraud.** If the communication was made, in whole or in part, to enable or aid anyone to commit or plan to commit a crime or fraud.

(B) Proceeding Between Spouses in Civil Cases. In (A) a proceeding brought by or on behalf of one spouse against the other spouse, or (B) a proceeding between a surviving spouse and a person who claims through the deceased spouse, regardless of whether the claim is by testate or intestate succession or by inter vivos transaction.

(C) Crime Against Spouse or Minor Child. In a proceeding in which the party is accused of conduct which, if proved, is a crime against the person of the spouse, any minor child, or any member of the household of either spouse.

(D) Commitment or Similar Proceeding. In a proceeding to commit either spouse or otherwise to place that person or that person's property, or both, under the control of another because of an alleged mental or physical condition.

(E) Proceeding to Establish Competence. In a proceeding brought by or on behalf of either spouse to establish competence.

(b) Privilege not to Testify in Criminal Case.

(1) Rule of privilege. In a criminal case, the spouse of the accused has a privilege not to be called as a witness for the state. This rule does not prohibit the spouse from testifying voluntarily for the state, even over objection by the accused. A spouse who testifies on behalf of an accused is subject to cross-examination as provided in rule 611(b).

(2) Failure to call as witness. Failure by an accused to call the accused's spouse as a witness, where other evidence indicates that the spouse could testify to relevant matters, is a proper subject of comment by counsel.

(3) Who may claim the privilege. The privilege not to testify may be claimed by the person or the person's guardian or representative but not by that person's spouse.

(4) Exceptions. The privilege of a person's spouse not to be called as a witness for the state does not apply:

(A) Certain criminal proceedings. In any proceeding in which the person is charged with a crime against the person's spouse, a member of the household of either spouse, or any minor.

(B) Matters occurring prior to marriage. As to matters occurring prior to the marriage.

RULE 505. COMMUNICATIONS TO MEMBERS OF THE CLERGY

(a) Definitions. As used in this rule:

(1) A "member of the clergy" is a minister, priest, rabbi, accredited Christian Science Practitioner, or other similar functionary of a religious organization or an individual reasonably believed so to be by the person consulting with such individual.

(2) A communication is "confidential" if made privately and not intended for further disclosure except to other persons present in furtherance of the purpose of the communication.

(b) General Rule of Privilege. A person has a privilege to refuse to disclose and to prevent another from disclosing a confidential communication by the person to a member of the clergy in the member's professional character as spiritual adviser.

(c) Who May Claim the Privilege. The privilege may be claimed by the person, by the person's guardian or conservator, or by the personal representative of the person if the person is deceased. The member of the clergy to whom the communication was made is presumed to have authority to claim the privilege but only on behalf of the communicant.

RULE 506. POLITICAL VOTE

Every person has a privilege to refuse to disclose the tenor of the person's vote at a political election conducted by secret ballot unless the vote was cast illegally.

RULE 507. TRADE SECRETS

A person has a privilege, which may be claimed by the person or the person's agent or employee, to refuse to disclose and to prevent other persons from disclosing a trade secret owned by the person, if the allowance of the privilege will not tend to conceal fraud or otherwise work injustice. When disclosure is directed, the judge shall take such protective measure as the interests of the holder of the privilege and of the parties and the furtherance of justice may require.

RULE 508. IDENTITY OF INFORMER

(a) Rule of Privilege. The United States or a state or subdivision thereof has a privilege to refuse to disclose the identity of a person who has furnished information relating to or assisting in an investigation of a possible violation of a law to a law enforcement officer or member of a legislative committee or its staff conducting an investigation.

(b) Who May Claim. The privilege may be claimed by an appropriate representative of the public entity to which the information was furnished, except the privilege shall not be allowed in criminal cases if the state objects.

(c) Exceptions.

(1) Voluntary disclosure; informer a witness. No privilege exists under this rule if the identity of the informer or the informer's interest in the subject matter of the communication has been disclosed to those who would have cause to resent the communication by a holder of the privilege or by the informer's own action, or if the informer appears as a witness for the public entity.

(2) Testimony on merits. If it appears from the evidence in the case or from other showing by a party that an informer may be able to give testimony necessary to a fair determination of a material issue on the merits in a civil case to which the public entity is a party, or on guilt or innocence in a criminal case, and the public entity invokes the privilege, the court shall give the public entity an opportunity to show in camera facts relevant to determining whether the informer can, in fact, supply that testimony. The showing will ordinarily be in the form of affidavits, but the court may direct that testimony be taken if it finds that the matter cannot be resolved satisfactorily upon affidavit. If the court finds that there is a reasonable probability that the informer can give the testimony, and the public entity elects not to disclose the informer's identity, the court in a civil case may make any order that justice requires, and in a criminal case shall, on motion of the defendant, and may, on the court's own motion, dismiss the charges as to which the testimony would relate. Evidence submitted to the court shall be sealed and preserved to be made available to the appellate court in the event of an appeal, and the contents shall not otherwise be revealed without consent of the public entity. All counsel and parties shall be permitted to be present at every stage of proceedings under this subdivision except a showing in camera, at which no counsel or party shall be permitted to be present.

(3) Legality of obtaining evidence. If information from an informer is relied upon to establish the legality of the means by which evidence was obtained and the court is not satisfied that the information was received from an informer reasonably believed to be reliable or credible, it may require the identity of the informer to be disclosed. The court shall, on request of the public entity, direct that the disclosure be made in camera. All counsel and parties concerned with the issue of legality shall be permitted to be present at every stage of proceedings under this subdivision except a disclosure in camera, at which no counsel or party shall be permitted to be present. If disclosure of the identity of the informer is made in camera, the record thereof shall be sealed and preserved to be made available to the appellate court in the event of an appeal, and the contents shall not otherwise be revealed without consent of the public entity.

RULE 509. PHYSICIAN-PATIENT PRIVILEGE

(a) Definitions. As used in this rule:

(1) A "patient" means any person who consults or is seen by a physician to receive medical care.

(2) A "physician" means a person licensed to practice medicine in any state or nation, or reasonably believed by the patient so to be.

(3) A communication is "confidential" if not intended to be disclosed to third persons other than those present to further the interest of the patient in the consultation, examination, or interview, or those reasonably necessary for the transmission of the communication, or those who are participating in the diagnosis and treatment under the direction of the physician, including members of the patient's family.

(b) Limited Privilege in Criminal Proceedings. There is no physician-patient privilege in criminal proceedings. However, a communication to any person involved in the treatment or examination of alcohol or drug abuse by a person being treated voluntarily or being examined for admission to treatment for alcohol or drug abuse is not admissible in a criminal proceeding.

(c) General Rule of Privilege in Civil Proceedings. In a civil proceeding:

(1) Confidential communications between a physician and a patient, relative to or in connection with any professional services rendered by a physician to the patient are privileged and may not be disclosed.

(2) Records of the identity, diagnosis, evaluation, or treatment of a patient by a physician that are created or maintained by a physician are confidential and privileged and may not be disclosed.

(3) The provisions of this rule apply even if the patient received the services of a physician prior to the enactment of the Medical Liability and Insurance Improvement Act, Tex. Rev. Civ. Stat. art. 4590i.

(d) Who May Claim the Privilege in a Civil Proceeding. In a civil proceeding:

(1) The privilege of confidentiality may be claimed by the patient or by a representative of the patient acting on the patient's behalf.

(2) The physician may claim the privilege of confidentiality, but only on behalf of the patient. The authority to do so is presumed in the absence of evidence to the contrary.

(e) Exceptions in a Civil Proceeding. Exceptions to confidentiality or privilege in administrative proceedings or in civil proceedings in court exist:

(1) when the proceedings are brought by the patient against a physician, including but not limited to malpractice proceedings, and in any license revocation proceeding in which the patient is a complaining witness and in which disclosure is relevant to the claims or defense of a physician;

(2) when the patient or someone authorized to act on the patient's behalf submits a written consent to the release of any privileged information, as provided in paragraph (f);

(3) when the purpose of the proceedings is to substantiate and collect on a claim for medical services rendered to the patient;

(4) as to a communication or record relevant to an issue of the physical, mental or emotional condition of a patient in any proceeding in which any party relies upon the condition as a part of the party's claim or defense;

(5) in any disciplinary investigation or proceeding of a physician conducted under or pursuant to the Medical Practice Act, Tex. Rev. Civ. Stat. art. 4495b, or of a registered nurse under or pursuant to Tex. Rev. Civ. Stat. arts. 4525, 4527a, 4527b, and 4527c, provided that the board shall protect the identity of any patient whose medical records are examined, except for those patients covered under subparagraph (e)(1) or those patients who have submitted written consent to the release of their medical records as provided by paragraph (f);

(6) in an involuntary civil commitment proceeding, proceeding for court-ordered treatment, or probable cause hearing under Tex. Health & Safety Code ch. 462; tit. 7, subtit. C; and tit. 7, subtit. D;

(7) in any proceeding regarding the abuse or neglect, or the cause of any abuse or neglect, of the resident of an "institution" as defined in Tex. Health & Safety Code §242.002.

(f) Consent.

(1) Consent for the release of privileged information must be in writing and signed by the patient, or a parent or legal guardian if the patient is a minor, or a legal guardian if the patient has been adjudicated incompetent to manage personal affairs, or an attorney ad litem appointed for the patient, as authorized by Tex. Health & Safety Code tit. 7, subtits. C and D; Tex. Prob. Code ch. V; and Tex. Fam. Code §107.011; or a personal representative if the patient is deceased, provided that the written consent specifies the following:

(A) the information or medical records to be covered by the release;

(B) the reasons or purposes for the release; and

(C) the person to whom the information is to be released.

(2) The patient, or other person authorized to consent, has the right to withdraw consent to the release of any information. Withdrawal of consent does not affect any information disclosed prior to the written notice of the withdrawal.

(3) Any person who received information made privileged by this rule may disclose the information to others only to the extent consistent with the authorized purposes for which consent to release the information was obtained.

RULE 510. CONFIDENTIALITY OF MENTAL HEALTH INFORMATION IN CIVIL CASES

(a) Definitions. As used in this rule:

(1) "Professional" means any person:

(A) authorized to practice medicine in any state or nation;

(B) licensed or certified by the State of Texas in the diagnosis, evaluation or treatment of any mental or emotional disorder;

(C) involved in the treatment or examination of drug abusers; or

(D) reasonably believed by the patient to be included in any of the preceding categories.

(2) "Patient" means any person who:

(A) consults, or is interviewed by, a professional for purposes of diagnosis, evaluation, or treatment of any mental or emotional condition or disorder, including alcoholism and drug addiction; or

(B) is being treated voluntarily or being examined for admission to voluntary treatment for drug abuse.

(3) A representative of the patient is:

(A) any person bearing the written consent of the patient;

(B) a parent if the patient is a minor;

(C) a guardian if the patient has been adjudicated incompetent to manage the patient's personal affairs; or

(D) the patient's personal representative if the patient is deceased.

(4) A communication is "confidential" if not intended to be disclosed to third persons other than those present to further the interest of the patient in the diagnosis, examination, evaluation, or treatment, or those reasonably necessary for the transmission of the communication, or those who are participating in the diagnosis, examination, evaluation, or treatment under the direction of the professional, including members of the patient's family.

(b) General Rule of Privilege.

(1) Communication between a patient and a professional is confidential and shall not be disclosed in civil cases.

(2) Records of the identity, diagnosis, evaluation, or treatment of a patient which are created or maintained by a professional are confidential and shall not be disclosed in civil cases.

(3) Any person who received information from confidential communications or records as defined herein, other than a representative of the patient acting on the patient's behalf, shall not disclose in civil cases the information except to the extent that disclosure is consistent with the authorized purposes for which the information was first obtained.

(4) The provisions of this rule apply even if the patient received the services of a professional prior to the enactment of Tex. Rev. Civ. Stat. art. 5561h (Vernon Supp. 1984) (now codified as Tex. Health & Safety Code §§ 611.001-611.008).

(c) Who May Claim the Privilege.

(1) The privilege of confidentiality may be claimed by the patient or by a representative of the patient acting on the patient's behalf.

(2) The professional may claim the privilege of confidentiality but only on behalf of the patient. The authority to do so is presumed in the absence of evidence to the contrary.

(d) Exceptions. Exceptions to the privilege in court or administrative proceedings exist:

(1) when the proceedings are brought by the patient against a professional, including but not limited to malpractice proceedings, and in any license revocation proceedings in which the patient is a complaining witness and in which disclosure is relevant to the claim or defense of a professional;

(2) when the patient waives the right in writing to the privilege of confidentiality of any information, or when a representative of the patient acting on the patient's behalf submits a written waiver to the confidentiality privilege;

(3) when the purpose of the proceeding is to substantiate and collect on a claim for mental or emotional health services rendered to the patient;

(4) when the judge finds that the patient after having been previously informed that communications would not be privileged, has made communications to a professional in the course of a court-ordered examination relating to the patient's mental or emotional condition or disorder, providing that such communications shall not be privileged only with respect to issues involving the patient's mental or emotional health. On granting of the order, the court, in determining the extent to which any disclosure of all or any part of any communication is necessary, shall impose appropriate safeguards against unauthorized disclosure;

(5) as to a communication or record relevant to an issue of the physical, mental or emotional condition of a patient in any proceeding in which any party relies upon the condition as a part of the party's claim or defense;

(6) in any proceeding regarding the abuse or neglect, or the cause of any abuse or neglect, of the resident of an institution as defined in Tex. Health and Safety Code §242.002.

RULE 511. WAIVER OF PRIVILEGE BY VOLUNTARY DISCLOSURE

A person upon whom these rules confer a privilege against disclosure waives the privilege if:

(1) the person or a predecessor of the person while holder of the privilege voluntarily discloses or consents to disclosure of any significant part of the privileged matter unless such disclosure itself is privileged; or

(2) the person or a representative of the person calls a person to whom privileged communications have been made to testify as to the person's character or character trait insofar as such communications are relevant to such character or character trait.

RULE 512. PRIVILEGED MATTER DISCLOSED UNDER COMPULSION OR WITHOUT OPPORTUNITY TO CLAIM PRIVILEGE

A claim of privilege is not defeated by a disclosure which was (1) compelled erroneously or (2) made without opportunity to claim the privilege.

RULE 513. COMMENT UPON OR INFERENCE FROM CLAIM OF PRIVILEGE; INSTRUCTION

(a) Comment or Inference Not Permitted. Except as permitted in Rule 504(b)(2), the claim of a privilege, whether in the present proceeding or upon a prior occasion, is not a proper subject of comment by judge or counsel, and no inference may be drawn therefrom.

(b) Claiming Privilege Without Knowledge of Jury. In jury cases, proceedings shall be conducted, to the extent practicable, so as to facilitate the making of claims of privilege without the knowledge of the jury.

(c) Claim of Privilege Against Self-Incrimination in Civil Cases. Paragraphs (a) and (b) shall not apply with respect to a party's claim, in the present civil proceeding, of the privilege against self-incrimination.

(d) Jury Instruction. Except as provided in Rule 504(b)(2) and in paragraph (c) of this Rule, upon request any party against whom the jury might draw an adverse inference from a claim of privilege is entitled to an instruction that no inference may be drawn therefrom.

ARTICLE VI. WITNESSES

RULE 601. COMPETENCY AND INCOMPETENCY OF WITNESSES

(a) General Rule. Every person is competent to be a witness except as otherwise provided in these rules. The following witnesses shall be incompetent to testify in any proceeding subject to these rules:

(1) Insane persons. Insane persons who, in the opinion of the court, are in an insane condition of mind at the time when they are offered as a witness, or who, in the opinion of the court, were in that condition when the events happened of which they are called to testify.

(2) Children. Children or other persons who, after being examined by the court, appear not to possess sufficient intellect to relate transactions with respect to which they are interrogated.

(b) "Dead Man's Rule" in Civil Actions. In civil actions by or against executors, administrators, or guardians, in which judgment may be rendered for or against them as such, neither party shall be allowed to testify against the others as to any oral statement by the testator, intestate or ward, unless that testimony to the oral statement is corroborated or unless the witness is called at the trial to testify thereto by the opposite party; and, the provisions of this article shall extend to and include all actions by or against the heirs or legal representatives of a decedent based in whole or in part on such oral statement. Except for the foregoing, a witness is not precluded from giving evidence of or concerning any transaction with, any conversations with, any admissions of, or statement by, a deceased or insane party or person merely because the witness is a party to the action or a person interested in the event thereof. The trial court shall, in a proper case, where this rule prohibits an interested party or witness from testifying, instruct the jury that such person is not permitted by the law to give evidence relating to any oral statement by the deceased or ward unless the oral statement is corroborated or unless the party or witness is called at the trial by the opposite party.

RULE 602. LACK OF PERSONAL KNOWLEDGE

A witness may not testify to a matter unless evidence is introduced sufficient to support a finding that the witness has personal knowledge of the matter. Evidence to prove personal knowledge may, but need not, consist of the testimony of the witness. This rule is subject to the provisions of Rule 703, relating to opinion testimony by expert witnesses.

RULE 603. OATH OR AFFIRMATION

Before testifying, every witness shall be required to declare that the witness will testify truthfully, by oath or affirmation administered in a form calculated to awaken the witness' conscience and impress the witness' mind with the duty to do so.

RULE 604. INTERPRETERS

An interpreter is subject to the provisions of these rules relating to qualification as an expert and the administration of an oath or affirmation to make a true translation.

RULE 605. COMPETENCY OF JUDGE AS A WITNESS

The judge presiding at the trial may not testify in that trial as a witness. No objection need be made in order to preserve the point.

RULE 606. COMPETENCY OF JUROR AS A WITNESS

(a) At the Trial. A member of the jury may not testify as a witness before that jury in the trial of the case in which the juror is sitting as a juror. If the juror is called so to testify, the opposing party shall be afforded an opportunity to object out of the presence of the jury.

(b) Inquiry Into Validity of Verdict or Indictment. Upon an inquiry into the validity of a verdict or indictment, a juror may not testify as to any matter or statement occurring during the jury's deliberations, or to the effect of anything on any juror's mind or emotions or mental processes, as influencing any juror's assent to or dissent from the verdict or indictment. Nor may a juror's affidavit or any statement by a juror concerning any matter about which the juror would be precluded from testifying be admitted in evidence for any of these purposes. However, a juror may testify: (1) whether any outside influence was improperly brought to bear upon any juror; or (2) to rebut a claim that the juror was not qualified to serve.

RULE 607. WHO MAY IMPEACH

The credibility of a witness may be attacked by any party, including the party calling the witness.

RULE 608. EVIDENCE OF CHARACTER AND CONDUCT OF A WITNESS

(a) Opinion and Reputation Evidence of Character. The credibility of a witness may be attacked or supported by evidence in the form of opinion or reputation, but subject to these limitations:

(1) the evidence may refer only to character for truthfulness or untruthfulness; and

(2) evidence of truthful character is admissible only after the character of the witness for truthfulness has been attacked by opinion or reputation evidence or otherwise.

(b) Specific Instances of Conduct. Specific instances of the conduct of a witness, for the purpose of attacking or supporting the witness' credibility, other than conviction of crime as provided in Rule 609, may not be inquired into on cross-examination of the witness nor proved by extrinsic evidence.

RULE 609. IMPEACHMENT BY EVIDENCE OF CONVICTION OF CRIME

(a) General Rule. For the purpose of attacking the credibility of a witness, evidence that the witness has been convicted of a crime shall be admitted if elicited from the witness or established by public record but only if the crime was a felony or involved moral turpitude, regardless of punishment, and the court determines that the probative value of admitting this evidence outweighs its prejudicial effect to a party.

(b) Time Limit. Evidence of a conviction under this rule is not admissible if a period of more than ten years has elapsed since the date of the conviction or of the release of the witness from the confinement imposed for that conviction, whichever is the later date, unless the court determines, in the interests of justice, that the probative value of the conviction supported by specific facts and circumstances substantially outweighs its prejudicial effect.

(c) Effect of Pardon, Annulment, or Certificate of Rehabilitation. Evidence of a conviction is not admissible under this rule if:

(1) based on the finding of the rehabilitation of the person convicted, the conviction has been the subject of a pardon, annulment, certificate of rehabilitation, or other equivalent procedure, and that person has not been convicted of a subsequent crime which was classified as a felony or involved moral turpitude, regardless of punishment;

(2) probation has been satisfactorily completed for the crime for which the person was convicted, and that person has not been convicted of a subsequent crime which was classified as a felony or involved moral turpitude, regardless of punishment; or

(3) based on a finding of innocence, the conviction has been the subject of a pardon, annulment, or other equivalent procedure.

(d) Juvenile Adjudications. Evidence of juvenile adjudications is not admissible, except for proceedings conducted pursuant to Title III, Family Code, in which the witness is a party, under this rule unless required to be admitted by the Constitution of the United States or Texas.

(e) Pendency of Appeal. Pendency of an appeal renders evidence of a conviction inadmissible.

(f) Notice. Evidence of a conviction is not admissible if after timely written request by the adverse party specifying the witness or witnesses, the proponent fails to give to the adverse party sufficient advance written notice of intent to use such evidence to provide the adverse party with a fair opportunity to contest the use of such evidence.

RULE 610. RELIGIOUS BELIEFS OR OPINIONS

Evidence of the beliefs or opinions of a witness on matters of religion is not admissible for the purpose of showing that by reason of their nature the witness' credibility is impaired or enhanced.

RULE 611. MODE AND ORDER OF INTERROGATION AND PRESENTATION

(a) Control by Court. The court shall exercise reasonable control over the mode and order of interrogating witnesses and presenting evidence so as to (1) make the interrogation and presentation effective for the ascertainment of the truth, (2) avoid needless consumption of time, and (3) protect witnesses from harassment or undue embarrassment.

(b) Scope of Cross-Examination. A witness may be cross-examined on any matter relevant to any issue in the case, including credibility.

(c) Leading Questions. Leading questions should not be used on the direct examination of a witness except as may be necessary to develop the testimony of the witness. Ordinarily leading questions should be permitted on cross-examination. When a party calls a hostile witness, an adverse party, or a witness identified with an adverse party, interrogation may be by leading questions.

RULE 612. WRITING USED TO REFRESH MEMORY

If a witness uses a writing to refresh memory for the purpose of testifying either

(1) while testifying;

(2) before testifying, in civil cases, if the court in its discretion determines it is necessary in the interests of justice; or

(3) before testifying, in criminal cases;

an adverse party is entitled to have the writing produced at the hearing, to inspect it, to cross-examine the witness thereon, and to introduce in evidence those portions which relate to the testimony of the witness. If it is claimed that the writing contains matters not related to the subject matter of the testimony the court shall examine the writing in camera, excise any portion not so related, and order delivery of the remainder to the party entitled thereto. Any portion withheld over objections shall be preserved and made available to the appellate court in the event of an appeal. If a writing is not produced or delivered pursuant to order under this rule, the court shall make any order justice requires, except that in criminal cases when the prosecution elects not to comply, the order shall be one striking the testimony or, if the court in its discretion determines that the interests of justice so require, declaring a mistrial.

RULE 613. PRIOR STATEMENTS OF WITNESSES: IMPEACHMENT AND SUPPORT

(a) Examining Witness Concerning Prior Inconsistent Statement. In examining a witness concerning a prior inconsistent statement made by the witness, whether oral or written, and before further cross-examination concerning, or extrinsic evidence of, such statement may be allowed, the witness must be told the contents of such statement and the time and place and the person to whom it was made, and must be afforded an opportunity to explain or deny such statement. If written, the writing need not be shown to the witness at that time, but on request the same shall be shown to opposing counsel. If the witness unequivocally admits having made such statement, extrinsic evidence of same shall not be admitted. This provision does not apply to admissions of a party-opponent as defined in Rule 801(e)(2).

(b) Examining Witness Concerning Bias or Interest. In impeaching a witness by proof of circumstances or statements showing bias or interest on the part of such witness, and before further cross-examination concerning, or extrinsic evidence of, such bias or interest may be allowed, the circumstances supporting such claim or the details of such statement, including the contents and where, when and to whom made, must be made known to the witness, and the witness must be given an opportunity to explain or to deny such circumstances or statement. If written, the writing need not be shown to the witness at that time, but on request the same shall be shown to opposing counsel. If the witness unequivocally admits such bias or interest, extrinsic evidence of same shall not be admitted. A party shall be permitted to present evidence rebutting any evidence impeaching one of said party's witnesses on grounds of bias or interest.

(c) Prior Consistent Statements of Witnesses. A prior statement of a witness which is consistent with the testimony of the witness is inadmissible except as provided in Rule 801(e)(1)(B).

RULE 614. EXCLUSION OF WITNESSES

At the request of a party the court shall order witnesses excluded so that they cannot hear the testimony of other witnesses, and it may make the order of its own motion. This rule does not authorize exclusion of:

(1) a party who is a natural person or in civil cases the spouse of such natural person;

(2) an officer or employee of a party in a civil case or a defendant in a criminal case that is not a natural person designated as its representative by its attorney;

(3) a person whose presence is shown by a party to be essential to the presentation of the party's cause; or

(4) the victim in a criminal case, unless the victim is to testify and the court determines that the victim's testimony would be materially affected if the victim hears other testimony at the trial.

RULE 615. PRODUCTION OF STATEMENTS OF WITNESSES IN CRIMINAL CASES

(a) Motion for Production. After a witness other than the defendant has testified on direct examination, the court, on motion of a party who did not call the witness, shall order the attorney for the state or the defendant and defendant's attorney, as the case may be, to produce, for the examination and use of the moving party, any statement of the witness that is in their possession and that relates to the subject matter concerning which the witness has testified.

(b) Production of Entire Statement. If the entire contents of the statement relate to the subject matter concerning which the witness has testified, the court shall order that the statement be delivered to the moving party.

(c) Production of Excised Statement. If the other party claims that the statement contains matter that does not relate to the subject matter concerning which the witness has testified, the court shall order that it be delivered to the court in camera. Upon inspection, the court shall excise the portions of the statement that do not relate to the subject matter concerning which the witness has testified, and shall order that the statement, with such material excised, be delivered to the moving party. Any portion withheld over objection shall be preserved and made available to the appellate court in the event of appeal.

(d) Recess for Examination of Statement. Upon delivery of the statement to the moving party, the court, upon application of that party, shall recess proceedings in the trial for a reasonable examination of such statement and for preparation for its use in the trial.

(e) Sanction for Failure to Produce Statement. If the other party elects not to comply with an order to deliver a statement to the moving party, the court shall order that the testimony of the witness be stricken from the record and that the trial proceed, or, if it is the attorney for the state who elects not to comply, shall declare a mistrial if required by the interest of justice.

(f) Definition. As used in this rule, a "statement" of a witness means:

(1) a written statement made by the witness that is signed or otherwise adopted or approved by the witness;

(2) a substantially verbatim recital of an oral statement made by the witness that is recorded contemporaneously with the making of the oral statement and that is contained in a stenographic, mechanical, electrical, or other recording or a transcription thereof; or

(3) a statement, however taken or recorded, or a transcription thereof, made by the witness to a grand jury.

ARTICLE VII. OPINIONS AND EXPERT TESTIMONY

RULE 701. OPINION TESTIMONY BY LAY WITNESSES

If the witness is not testifying as an expert, the witness' testimony in the form of opinions or inferences is limited to those opinions or inferences which are (a) rationally based on the perception of the witness and (b) helpful to a clear understanding of the witness' testimony or the determination of a fact in issue.

RULE 702. TESTIMONY BY EXPERTS

If scientific, technical, or other specialized knowledge will assist the trier of fact to understand the evidence or to determine a fact in issue, a witness qualified as an expert by knowledge, skill, experience, training, or education may testify thereto in the form of an opinion or otherwise.

RULE 703. BASES OF OPINION TESTIMONY BY EXPERTS

The facts or data in the particular case upon which an expert bases an opinion or inference may be those perceived by, reviewed by, or made known to the expert at or before the hearing. If of a type reasonably relied upon by experts in the particular field in forming opinions or inferences upon the subject, the facts or data need not be admissible in evidence.

RULE 704. OPINION ON ULTIMATE ISSUE

Testimony in the form of an opinion or inference otherwise admissible is not objectionable because it embraces an ultimate issue to be decided by the trier of fact.

RULE 705. DISCLOSURE OF FACTS OR DATA UNDERLYING EXPERT OPINION

(a) Disclosure of Facts or Data. The expert may testify in terms of opinion or inference and give the expert's reasons therefor without prior disclosure of the underlying facts or data, unless the court requires otherwise. The expert may in any event disclose on direct examination, or be required to disclose on cross-examination, the underlying facts or data.

(b) Voir Dire. Prior to the expert giving the expert's opinion or disclosing the underlying facts or data, a party against whom the opinion is offered upon request in a criminal case shall, or in a civil case may, be permitted to conduct a voir dire examination directed to the underlying facts or data upon which the opinion is based. This examination shall be conducted out of the hearing of the jury.

(c) Admissibility of Opinion. If the court determines that the underlying facts or data do not provide a sufficient basis for the expert's opinion under Rule 702 or 703, the opinion is inadmissible.

(d) Balancing Test; Limiting Instructions. When the underlying facts or data would be inadmissible in evidence, the court shall exclude the underlying facts or data if the danger that they will be used for a purpose other than as explanation or support for the expert's opinion outweighs their value as explanation or support or are unfairly prejudicial. If otherwise inadmissible facts or data are disclosed before the jury, a limiting instruction by the court shall be given upon request.

RULE 706. AUDIT IN CIVIL CASES

Despite any other evidence rule to the contrary, verified reports of auditors prepared pursuant to Rule of Civil Procedure 172, whether in the form of summaries, opinions, or otherwise, shall be admitted in evidence when offered by any party whether or not the facts or data in the reports are otherwise admissible and whether or not the reports embrace the ultimate issues to be decided by the trier of fact. Where exceptions to the reports have been filed, a party may contradict the reports by evidence supporting the exceptions.

ARTICLE VIII. HEARSAY

RULE 801. DEFINITIONS

The following definitions apply under this article:

(a) Statement. A "statement" is (1) an oral or written verbal expression or (2) nonverbal conduct of a person, if it is intended by the person as a substitute for verbal expression.

(b) Declarant. A "declarant" is a person who makes a statement.

(c) Matter Asserted. "Matter asserted" includes any matter explicitly asserted, and any matter implied by a statement, if the probative value of the statement as offered flows from declarant's belief as to the matter.

(d) Hearsay. "Hearsay" is a statement, other than one made by the declarant while testifying at the trial or hearing, offered in evidence to prove the truth of the matter asserted.

(e) Statements Which Are Not Hearsay. A statement is not hearsay if:

(1) Prior statement by witness. The declarant testifies at the trial or hearing and is subject to cross-examination concerning the statement, and the statement is:

(A) inconsistent with the declarant's testimony, and was given under oath subject to the penalty of perjury at a trial, hearing, or other proceeding except a grand jury proceeding in a criminal case, or in a deposition;

(B) consistent with the declarant's testimony and is offered to rebut an express or implied charge against the declarant of recent fabrication or improper influence or motive;

(C) one of identification of a person made after perceiving the person; or

(D) taken and offered in a criminal case in accordance with Code of Criminal Procedure article 38.071.

(2) Admission by party-opponent. The statement is offered against a party and is:

(A) the party's own statement in either an individual or representative capacity;

(B) a statement of which the party has manifested an adoption or belief in its truth;

(C) a statement by a person authorized by the party to make a statement concerning the subject;

(D) a statement by the party's agent or servant concerning a matter within the scope of the agency or employment, made during the existence of the relationship; or

(E) a statement by a co-conspirator of a party during the course and in furtherance of the conspiracy.

(3) Depositions. In a civil case, it is a deposition taken in the same proceeding, as same proceeding is defined in Rule of Civil Procedure 203.6(b). Unavailability of deponent is not a requirement for admissibility.

RULE 802. HEARSAY RULE

Hearsay is not admissible except as provided by statute or these rules or by other rules prescribed pursuant to statutory authority. Inadmissible hearsay admitted without objection shall not be denied probative value merely because it is hearsay.

RULE 803. HEARSAY EXCEPTIONS; AVAILABILITY OF DECLARANT IMMATERIAL

The following are not excluded by the hearsay rule, even though the declarant is available as a witness:

(1) Present Sense Impression. A statement describing or explaining an event or condition made while the declarant was perceiving the event or condition, or immediately thereafter.

(2) Excited Utterance. A statement relating to a startling event or condition made while the declarant was under the stress of excitement caused by the event or condition.

(3) Then Existing Mental, Emotional, or Physical Condition. A statement of the declarant's then existing state of mind, emotion, sensation, or physical condition (such as intent, plan, motive, design, mental feeling, pain, or bodily health), but not including a statement of memory or belief to prove the fact remembered or believed unless it relates to the execution, revocation, identification, or terms of declarant's will.

(4) Statements for Purposes of Medical Diagnosis or Treatment. Statements made for purposes of medical diagnosis or treatment and describing medical history, or past or present symptoms, pain, or sensations, or the inception or general character of the cause or external source thereof insofar as reasonably pertinent to diagnosis or treatment.

(5) Recorded Recollection. A memorandum or record concerning a matter about which a witness once had personal knowledge but now has insufficient recollection to enable the witness to testify fully and accurately, shown to have been made or adopted by the witness when the matter was fresh in the witness' memory and to reflect that knowledge correctly, unless the circumstances of preparation cast doubt on the document's trustworthiness. If admitted, the memorandum or record may be read into evidence but may not itself be received as an exhibit unless offered by an adverse party.

(6) Records of Regularly Conducted Activity. A memorandum, report, record, or data compilation, in any form, of acts, events, conditions, opinions, or diagnoses, made at or near the time by, or from information transmitted by, a person with knowledge, if kept in the course of a regularly conducted business activity, and if it was the regular practice of that business activity to make the memorandum, report, record, or data compilation, all as shown by the testimony of the custodian or other qualified witness, or by affidavit that complies with Rule 902(10), unless the source of information or the method or circumstances of preparation indicate lack of trustworthiness. "Business" as used in this paragraph includes any and every kind of regular organized activity whether conducted for profit or not.

(7) Absence of Entry in Records Kept in Accordance With the Provisions of Paragraph (6). Evidence that a matter is not included in the memoranda, reports, records, or data compilations, in any form, kept in accordance with the provisions of paragraph (6), to prove the nonoccurrence or nonexistence of the matter, if the matter was of a kind of which a memorandum, report, record, or data compilation was regularly made and preserved, unless the sources of information or other circumstances indicate lack of trustworthiness.

(8) Public Records and Reports. Records, reports, statements, or data compilations, in any form, of public offices or agencies setting forth:

(A) the activities of the office or agency;

(B) matters observed pursuant to duty imposed by law as to which matters there was a duty to report, excluding in criminal cases matters observed by police officers and other law enforcement personnel; or

(C) in civil cases as to any party and in criminal cases as against the state, factual findings resulting from an investigation made pursuant to authority granted by law;

unless the sources of information or other circumstances indicate lack of trustworthiness.

(9) Records of Vital Statistics. Records or data compilations, in any form, of births, fetal deaths, deaths, or marriages, if the report thereof was made to a public office pursuant to requirements of law.

(10) Absence of Public Record or Entry. To prove the absence of a record, report, statement, or data compilation, in any form, or the nonoccurrence or nonexistence of a matter of which a record, report, statement, or data compilation, in any form, was regularly made and preserved by a public office or agency, evidence in the form of a certification in accordance with Rule 902, or testimony, that diligent search failed to disclose the record, report statement, or data compilation, or entry.

(11) Records of Religious Organizations. Statements of births, marriages, divorces, deaths, legitimacy, ancestry, relationship by blood or marriage, or other similar facts of personal or family history, contained in a regularly kept record of a religious organization.

(12) Marriage, Baptismal, and Similar Certificates. Statements of fact contained in a certificate that the maker performed a marriage or other ceremony or administered a sacrament, made by a member of the clergy, public official, or other person authorized by the rules or practices of a religious organization or by law to perform the act certified, and purporting to have been issued at the time of the act or within a reasonable time thereafter.

(13) Family Records. Statements of fact concerning personal or family history contained in family Bibles, genealogies, charts, engravings on rings, inscriptions on family portraits, engravings on urns, crypts, or tombstones, or the like.

(14) Records of Documents Affecting an Interest in Property. The record of a document purporting to establish or affect an interest in property, as proof of the content of the original recorded document and its execution and delivery by each person by whom it purports to have been executed, if the record is a record of a public office and an applicable statute authorizes the recording of documents of that kind in that office.

(15) Statements in Documents Affecting an Interest in Property. A statement contained in a document purporting to establish or affect an interest in property if the matter stated was relevant to the purpose of the document, unless dealings with the property since the document was made have been inconsistent with the truth of the statement or the purport of the document.

(16) Statements in Ancient Documents. Statements in a document in existence twenty years or more the authenticity of which is established.

(17) Market Reports, Commercial Publications. Market quotations, tabulations, lists, directories, or other published compilations, generally used and relied upon by the public or by persons in particular occupations.

(18) Learned Treatises. To the extent called to the attention of an expert witness upon cross-examination or relied upon by the expert in direct examination, statements contained in published treatises, periodicals, or pamphlets on a subject of history, medicine, or other science or art established as a reliable authority by the testimony or admission of the witness or by other expert testimony or by judicial notice. If admitted, the statements may be read into evidence but may not be received as exhibits.

(19) Reputation Concerning Personal or Family History. Reputation among members of a person's family by blood, adoption, or marriage, or among a person's associates, or in the community, concerning a person's birth, adoption, marriage, divorce, death, legitimacy, relationship by blood, adoption, or marriage, ancestry, or other similar fact of personal or family history.

(20) Reputation Concerning Boundaries or General History. Reputation in a community, arising before the controversy, as to boundaries of or customs affecting lands in the community, and reputation as to events of general history important to the community or state or nation in which located.

(21) Reputation as to Character. Reputation of a person's character among associates or in the community.

(22) Judgment of Previous Conviction. In civil cases, evidence of a judgment, entered after a trial or upon a plea of guilty (but not upon a plea of nolo contendere), judging a person guilty of a felony, to prove any fact essential to sustain the judgment of conviction. In criminal cases, evidence of a judgment, entered after a trial or upon a plea of guilty or nolo contendere, adjudging a person guilty of a criminal offense, to prove any fact essential to sustain the judgment of conviction, but not including, when offered by the state for purposes other than impeachment, judgments against persons other than the accused. In all cases, the pendency of an appeal renders such evidence inadmissible.

(23) Judgment as to Personal, Family, or General History, or Boundaries. Judgments as proof of matters of personal, family or general history, or boundaries, essential to the judgment, if the same would be provable by evidence of reputation.

(24) Statement Against Interest. A statement which was at the time of its making so far contrary to the declarant's pecuniary or proprietary interest, or so far tended to subject the declarant to civil or criminal liability, or to render invalid a claim by the declarant against another, or to make the declarant an object of hatred, ridicule, or disgrace, that a reasonable person in declarant's position would not have made the statement unless believing it to be true. In criminal cases, a statement tending to expose the declarant to criminal liability is not admissible unless corroborating circumstances clearly indicate the trustworthiness of the statement.

RULE 804. HEARSAY EXCEPTIONS; DECLARANT UNAVAILABLE

(a) Definition of Unavailability. "Unavailability as a witness" includes situations in which the declarant:

(1) is exempted by ruling of the court on the ground of privilege from testifying concerning the subject matter of the declarant's statement;

(2) persists in refusing to testify concerning the subject matter of the declarant's statement despite an order of the court to do so;

(3) testifies to a lack of memory of the subject matter of the declarant's statement;

(4) is unable to be present or to testify at the hearing because of death or then existing physical or mental illness or infirmity; or

(5) is absent from the hearing and the proponent of the declarant's statement has been unable to procure the declarant's attendance or testimony by process or other reasonable means.

A declarant is not unavailable as a witness if the declarant's exemption, refusal, claim of lack of memory, inability, or absence is due to the procurement or wrong-doing of the proponent of the declarant's statement for the purpose of preventing the witness from attending or testifying.

(b) Hearsay Exceptions. The following are not excluded if the declarant is unavailable as a witness:

(1) Former testimony. In civil cases, testimony given as a witness at another hearing of the same or a different proceeding, or in a deposition taken in the course of another proceeding, if the party against whom the testimony is now offered, or a person with a similar interest, had an opportunity and similar motive to develop the testimony by direct, cross, or redirect examination. In criminal cases, testimony given as a witness at another hearing of the same or a different proceeding, if the party against whom the testimony is now offered had an opportunity and similar motive to develop the testimony by direct, cross, or redirect examination. In criminal cases the use of depositions is controlled by Chapter 39 of the Code of Criminal Procedure.

(2) Dying declarations. A statement made by a declarant while believing that the declarant's death was imminent, concerning the cause or circumstances of what the declarant believed to be impending death.

(3) Statement of personal or family history.

(A) A statement concerning the declarant's own birth, adoption, marriage, divorce, legitimacy, relationship by blood, adoption, or marriage, ancestry, or other similar fact of personal or family history even though declarant had no means of acquiring personal knowledge of the matter stated; or

(B) A statement concerning the foregoing matters, and death also, of another person, if the declarant was related to the other by blood, adoption, or marriage or was so intimately associated with the other's family as to be likely to have accurate information concerning the matter declared.

RULE 805. HEARSAY WITHIN HEARSAY

Hearsay included within hearsay is not excluded under the hearsay rule if each part of the combined statements conforms with an exception to the hearsay rule provided in these rules.

RULE 806. ATTACKING AND SUPPORTING CREDIBILITY OF DECLARANT

When a hearsay statement, or a statement defined in Rule 801(e)(2)(C), (D), or (E), or in civil cases a statement defined in Rule 801(e)(3), has been admitted in evidence, the credibility of the declarant may be attacked, and if attacked may be supported by any evidence which would be admissible for those purposes if declarant had testified as a witness. Evidence of a statement or conduct by the declarant at any time, offered to impeach the declarant, is not subject to any requirement that the declarant may have been afforded an opportunity to deny or explain. If the party against whom a hearsay statement has been admitted calls the declarant as a witness, the party is entitled to examine the declarant on the statement as if under cross-examination.

ARTICLE IX. AUTHENTICATION AND IDENTIFICATION

RULE 901. REQUIREMENT OF AUTHENTICATION OR IDENTIFICATION

(a) General Provision. The requirement of authentication or identification as a condition precedent to admissibility is satisfied by evidence sufficient to support a finding that the matter in question is what its proponent claims.

(b) Illustrations. By way of illustration only, and not by way of limitation, the following are examples of authentication or identification conforming with the requirements of this rule:

(1) Testimony of witness with knowledge. Testimony that a matter is what it is claimed to be.

(2) Nonexpert opinion on handwriting. Nonexpert opinion as to the genuineness of handwriting, based upon familiarity not acquired for purposes of the litigation.

(3) Comparison by trier or expert witness. Comparison by the trier of fact or by expert witness with specimens which have been found by the court to be genuine.

(4) Distinctive characteristics and the like. Appearance, contents, substance, internal patterns, or other distinctive characteristics, taken in conjunction with circumstances.

(5) Voice identification. Identification of a voice, whether heard firsthand or through mechanical or electronic transmission or recording, by opinion based upon hearing the voice at anytime under circumstances connecting it with the alleged speaker.

(6) Telephone conversations. Telephone conversations, by evidence that a call was made to the number assigned at the time by the telephone company to a particular person or business, if:

(A) in the case of a person, circumstances, including self-identification, show the person answering to be the one called; or

(B) in the case of a business, the call was made to a place of business and the conversation related to business reasonably transacted over the telephone.

(7) Public records or reports. Evidence that a writing authorized by law to be recorded or filed and in fact recorded or filed in a public office, or a purported public record, report, statement, or data compilation, in any form, is from the public office where items of this nature are kept.

(8) Ancient documents or data compilation. Evidence that a document or data compilation, in any form, (A) is in such condition as to create no suspicion concerning its authenticity, (B) was in a place where it, if authentic, would likely be, and (C) has been in existence twenty years or more at the time it is offered.

(9) Process or system. Evidence describing a process or system used to produce a result and showing that the process or system produces an accurate result.

(10) Methods provided by statute or rule. Any method of authentication or identification provided by statute or by other rule prescribed pursuant to statutory authority.

RULE 902. SELF-AUTHENTICATION

Extrinsic evidence of authenticity as a condition precedent to admissibility is not required with respect to the following:

(1) Domestic Public Documents Under Seal. A document bearing a seal purporting to be that of the United States, or of any State, district, Commonwealth, territory, or insular possession thereof, or the Panama Canal Zone, or the Trust Territory of the Pacific Islands, or of a political subdivision, department, officer, or agency thereof, and a signature purporting to be an attestation or execution.

(2) Domestic Public Documents Not Under Seal. A document purporting to bear the signature in the official capacity of an officer or employee of any entity included in paragraph (1) hereof, having no seal, if a public officer having a seal and having official duties in the district or political subdivision of the officer or employee certifies under seal that the signer has the official capacity and that the signature is genuine.

(3) Foreign Public Documents. A document purporting to be executed or attested in an official capacity by a person, authorized by the laws of a foreign country to make the execution or attestation, and accompanied by a final certification as to the genuineness of the signature and official position (A) of the executing or attesting person, or (B) of any foreign official whose certificate of genuineness of signature and official position relates to the execution or attestation or is in a chain of certificates of genuineness of signature and official position relating to the execution or attestation. A final certification may be made by a secretary of embassy or legation, consul general, consul, vice consul, or consular agent of the United States, or a diplomatic or consular official of the foreign country assigned or accredited to the United States. If reasonable opportunity has been given to all parties to investigate the authenticity and accuracy of official documents, the court may, for good cause shown, order that they be treated as presumptively authentic without final certification or permit them to be evidenced by an attested summary with or without final certification. The final certification shall be dispensed with whenever both the United

States and the foreign country in which the official record is located are parties to a treaty or convention that abolishes or displaces such requirement, in which case the record and the attestation shall be certified by the means provided in the treaty or convention.

(4) Certified Copies of Public Records. A copy of an official record or report or entry therein, or of a document authorized by law to be recorded or filed and actually recorded or filed in a public office, including data compilations in any form certified as correct by the custodian or other person authorized to make the certification, by certificate complying with paragraph (1), (2) or (3) of this rule or complying with any statute or other rule prescribed pursuant to statutory authority.

(5) Official Publications. Books, pamphlets, or other publications purporting to be issued by public authority.

(6) Newspapers and Periodicals. Printed materials purporting to be newspapers or periodicals.

(7) Trade Inscriptions and the Like. Inscriptions, signs, tags, or labels purporting to have been affixed in the course of business and indicating ownership, control, or origin.

(8) Acknowledged Documents. Documents accompanied by a certificate of acknowledgment executed in the manner provided by law by a notary public or other officer authorized by law to take acknowledgments.

(9) Commercial Paper and Related Documents. Commercial paper, signatures thereon, and documents relating thereto to the extent provided by general commercial law.

(10) Business Records Accompanied by Affidavit.

(a) Records or Photocopies; Admissibility; Affidavit; Filing. Any record or set of records or photographically reproduced copies of such records, which would be admissible under Rule 803(6) or (7) shall be admissible in evidence in any court in this state upon the affidavit of the person who would otherwise provide the prerequisites of Rule 803(6) or (7), that such records attached to such affidavit were in fact so kept as required by Rule 803(6) or (7), provided further, that such record or records along with such affidavit are filed with the clerk of the court for inclusion with the papers in the cause in which the record or records are sought to be used as evidence at least fourteen days prior to the day upon which trial of said cause commences, and provided the other parties to said cause are given prompt notice by the party filing same of the filing of such record or records and affidavit, which notice shall identify the name and employer, if any, of the person making the affidavit and such records shall be made available to the counsel for other parties to the action or litigation for inspection and copying. The expense for copying shall be borne by the party, parties or persons who desire copies and not by the party or parties who file the records and serve notice of said filing, in compliance with this rule. Notice shall be deemed to have been promptly given if it is served in the manner contemplated by Rule of Civil Procedure 21(a) fourteen days prior to commencement of trial in said cause.

(b) Form of Affidavit. A form for the affidavit of such person as shall make such affidavit as is permitted in paragraph (a) above shall be sufficient if it follows this form though this form shall not be exclusive, and an affidavit which substantially complies with the provisions of this rule shall suffice, to-wit:

No. ______________

John Doe	§	IN THE __________
(Name of Plaintiff)	§	COURT IN AND FOR
v.	§	________ COUNTY,
John Roe	§	TEXAS
(Name of Defendant)	§	

AFFIDAVIT

Before me, the undersigned authority, personally appeared ______, who, being by me duly sworn, deposed as follows:

My name is ______, I am of sound mind, capable of making this affidavit, and personally acquainted with the facts herein stated:

I am the custodian of the records of ______. Attached hereto are ____ pages of records from ______. These said ___ pages of records are kept by ______ in the regular course of business, and it was the regular course of business of _____ for an employee or representative of _____, with knowledge of the act, event, condition, opinion, or diagnosis, recorded to make the record or to transmit information thereof to be included in such record; and the record was made at or near the time or reasonably soon thereafter. The records attached hereto are the original or exact duplicates of the original.

____

Affiant

SWORN TO AND SUBSCRIBED before me on the _________ day of _________, 19 ____.

____

Notary Public, State of Texas

Notary's printed name:

____

My commission expires:

____

(11) Presumptions Under Statutes or Other Rules. Any signature, document, or other matter declared by statute or by other rules prescribed pursuant to statutory authority to be presumptively or prima facie genuine or authentic.

RULE 903. SUBSCRIBING WITNESS' TESTIMONY UNNECESSARY

The testimony of a subscribing witness is not necessary to authenticate a writing unless required by the laws of the jurisdiction whose laws govern the validity of the writing.

ARTICLE X. CONTENTS OF WRITINGS, RECORDINGS, AND PHOTOGRAPHS

RULE 1001. DEFINITIONS

For purposes of this article the following definitions are applicable:

(a) Writings and Recordings. "Writings" and "recordings" consist of letters, words, or numbers or their equivalent, set down by handwriting, typewriting, printing, photostating, photographing, magnetic impulse, mechanical or electronic recording, or other form of data compilation.

(b) Photographs. "Photographs" include still photographs, X-ray films, video tapes, and motion pictures.

(c) Original. An "original" of a writing or recording is the writing or recording itself or any counterpart intended to have the same effect by a person executing or issuing it. An "original" of a photograph includes the negative or any print therefrom. If data are stored in a computer or similar device, any printout or other output readable by sight, shown to reflect the data accurately, is an "original."

(d) Duplicate. A "duplicate" is a counterpart produced by the same impression as the original, or from the same matrix, or by means of photography, including enlargements and miniatures, or by mechanical or electronic re-recording, or by chemical reproduction, or by other equivalent techniques which accurately reproduce the original.

RULE 1002. REQUIREMENT OF ORIGINALS

To prove the content of a writing, recording, or photograph, the original writing, recording, or photograph is required except as otherwise provided in these rules or by law.

RULE 1003. ADMISSIBILITY OF DUPLICATES

A duplicate is admissible to the same extent as an original unless (1) a question is raised as to the authenticity of the original or (2) in the circumstances it would be unfair to admit the duplicate in lieu of the original.

RULE 1004. ADMISSIBILITY OF OTHER EVIDENCE OF CONTENTS

The original is not required, and other evidence of the contents of a writing, recording, or photograph is admissible if:

(a) Originals Lost or Destroyed. All originals are lost or have been destroyed, unless the proponent lost or destroyed them in bad faith;

(b) Original Not Obtainable. No original can be obtained by any available judicial process or procedure;

(c) Original Outside the State. No original is located in Texas;

(d) Original in Possession of Opponent. At a time when an original was under the control of the party against whom offered, that party was put on notice, by the pleadings or otherwise, that the content would be a subject of proof at the hearing, and that party does not produce the original at the hearing; or

(e) Collateral Matters. The writing, recording or photograph is not closely related to a controlling issue.

RULE 1005. PUBLIC RECORDS

The contents of an official record or of a document authorized to be recorded or filed and actually recorded or filed, including data compilations in any form, if otherwise admissible, may be proved by copy, certified as correct in accordance with Rule 902 or testified to be correct by a witness who has compared it with the original. If a copy which complies with the foregoing cannot be obtained by the exercise of reasonable diligence, then other evidence of the contents may be given.

RULE 1006. SUMMARIES

The contents of voluminous writings, recordings, or photographs, otherwise admissible, which cannot conveniently be examined in court may be presented in the form of a chart, summary, or calculation. The originals, or duplicates, shall be made available for examination or copying, or both, by other parties at a reasonable time and place. The court may order that they be produced in court.

RULE 1007. TESTIMONY OR WRITTEN ADMISSION OF PARTY

Contents of writings, recordings, or photographs may be proved by the testimony or deposition of the party against whom offered or by that party's written admission, without accounting for the nonproduction of the original.

RULE 1008. FUNCTIONS OF COURT AND JURY

When the admissibility of other evidence of contents of writings, recordings, or photographs under these rules depends upon the fulfillment of a condition of fact, the question whether the condition has been fulfilled is ordinarily for the court to determine in accordance with the provisions of Rule 104. However, when an issue is raised (a) whether the asserted writing ever existed, or (b) whether another writing, recording, or photograph produced at the trial is the original, or (c) whether other evidence of contents correctly reflects the contents, the issue is for the trier of fact to determine as in the case of other issues of fact.

RULE 1009. TRANSLATION OF FOREIGN LANGUAGE DOCUMENTS

(a) Translations. A translation of foreign language documents shall be admissible upon the affidavit of a qualified translator setting forth the qualifications of the translator and certifying that the translation is fair and accurate. Such affidavit, along with the translation and the underlying foreign language documents, shall be served upon all parties at least 45 days prior to the date of trial.

(b) Objections. Any party may object to the accuracy of another party's translation by pointing out the specific inaccuracies of the translation and by stating with specificity what the objecting party contends is a fair and accurate translation. Such objection shall be served upon all parties at least 15 days prior to the date of trial.

(c) Effect of Failure to Object or Offer Conflicting Translation. If no conflicting translation or objection is timely served, the court shall admit a translation submitted under paragraph (a) without need of proof, provided however that the underlying foreign language documents are otherwise admissible under the Texas Rules of Evidence. Failure to serve a conflicting translation under paragraph (a) or failure to timely and properly object to the accuracy of a translation under paragraph (b) shall preclude a party from attacking or offering evidence contradicting the accuracy of such translation at trial.

(d) Effect of Objections or Conflicting Translations. In the event of conflicting translations under paragraph (a) or if objections to another party's translation are served under paragraph (b), the court shall determine whether there is a genuine issue as to the accuracy of a material part of the translation to be resolved by the trier of fact.

(e) Expert Testimony of Translator. Except as provided in paragraph (c), this Rule does not preclude the admission of a translation of foreign language documents at trial either by live testimony or by deposition testimony of a qualified expert translator.

(f) Varying of Time Limits. The court, upon motion of any party and for good cause shown, may enlarge or shorten the time limits set forth in this Rule.

(g) Court Appointment. The court, if necessary, may appoint a qualified translator, the reasonable value of whose services shall be taxed as court costs.